THE BLIND MEN AND THE ELEPHANT

THE BLIND MEN
AND THE ELEPHANT

Mastering Project Work

How to
Transform
Fuzzy
Responsibilities
Into Meaningful
Results

DAVID A. SCHMALTZ

ILLUSTRATIONS BY D. WILDER SCHMALTZ

BK

BERRETT-KOEHLER PUBLISHERS, INC.
San Francisco
www.bkconnection.com

Berrett-Koehler Publishers, Inc.
235 Montgomery Street, Suite 650
San Francisco, CA 94104-2916
Tel: (415) 288-0260   Fax: (415) 362-2512   www.bkconnection.com

Ordering Information
Quantity sales. Special discounts are available on quantity purchases by corporations, associations, and others. For details, contact the "Special Sales Department" at the Berrett-Koehler address above.
Individual sales. Berrett-Koehler publications are available through most bookstores. They can also be ordered direct from Berrett-Koehler: Tel: (800) 929-2929; fax: (802) 864-7626; www.bkconnection.com.
Orders for college textbook/course adoption use. Please contact Berrett-Koehler: Tel: (800) 929-2929; fax: (802) 864-7626.
Orders by U.S. trade bookstores and wholesalers. Please contact Publishers Group West, 1700 Fourth Street, Berkeley, CA 94710. Tel: (510) 528-1444; fax (510) 528-3444.

Berrett-Koehler and the BK logo are registered trademarks of Berrett-Koehler Publishers, Inc.

Printed in the United States of America

Berrett-Koehler books are printed on long-lasting acid-free paper. When it is available, we choose paper that has been manufactured by environmentally responsible processes. These may include using trees grown in sustainable forests, incorporating recycled paper, minimizing chlorine in bleaching, or recycling the energy produced at the paper mill.

Library of Congress Cataloging-in-Publication Data

Schmaltz, David, 1951-
    The blind men and the elephant : mastering project work / by David Schmaltz.
        p. cm.
    Includes bibliographical references and index.
    ISBN 1-57675-253-4
    1. Project management. I. Title.

    HD69.P75 S36 2002
    658.4'04—dc21

                                                    2002038270

First Edition
08 07 06 05   10 9 8 7 6 5 4 3 2

Copyediting by Elissa Rabellino
Indexing by Rachel Rice
Cover and interior design and production by Bookwrights Design

DEDICATION

This book started as a series of letters to my then-future wife and business partner, Amy Schwab. I intended it to be a gift, presenting the earliest draft on her birthday. I dedicate this curious volume to Amy, who by all rights owns the manuscript. Amy found me spouting dangerously sane heresies and abandoned her own theologic wars to enter the conversation. I share these musings with her loving permission and the same unflagging encouragement that first prompted me to set fingers to keyboard.

—David A. Schmaltz

CONTENTS

PREFACE
NAIVE BEGINNINGS

. . . .

I don't know where to begin. I never do. My friend and teacher Dani Weinberg told me that the best defense against others' discovering something upsetting about me is to simply feature it, so I'm featuring it.

If you hope this book will tell you how to create successful projects, I want to disappoint you here. After all, if I can't disappoint you now, I'm unlikely to delight you later. I have not written this book to tell anyone what to do. Instead, I've written it with the idea of helping you discover and use what you already know. I've chosen this objective rather than the more common one of simply telling you what to do because I don't know what you should do. However, I believe that you probably already know most of what you need to know to create better projects. I have considerable practice helping others see their own experiences in more useful ways, so that's my objective here.

I intend to make some potentially shocking suggestions in this book. In a later chapter I will most outrageously suggest that you are presently powerful enough to transform your project work into something personally juicy. If you have no track record of creating such juiciness, my suggestions could either disturb or encourage you. I cannot know how you'll react. I want to warn you here, though, before you invest too much time reading this book, that by the time you finish reading it, you might discover some previously unknown sources of personal power and authority. This sort of discovery has always been and always will be dicey.

I've chosen to build this book out of stories. I think of these stories as parables rather than instructions. Parables are different from instructions in at least one very important way: While instructions present key learning points—what you should embrace or avoid—parables don't insist that you carry away any specific meaning from them. One day the parable might seem to mean one thing and another day something quite opposite. To me, this feature more closely tracks how the real world presents information, and since I can have no idea of your situation, we're probably both better off with this tactic than one where I pose as the expert and you as the novice. You're more experienced than a novice, and I'm expert enough to know that I'm not anybody else's expert. You are unavoidably the expert of your own experiences.

I'm writing this book to describe something that cannot be rationally explained: How is it that people continue engaging in project work, even though projects rarely meet their stated objectives? Our methods for making successful projects seem to take the soul out of them. Our insistence on planning straight and narrow pathways into the future frustrates the most expert among us, yet we persist.

I believe we persist because we either have experienced or aspire to encounter what I call *coherence*. Coherence is that state where we see the world through each other's eyes—where we quite magically catch ourselves seeing the world as others see it. Operational work separates tasks into isolated, homogeneous pieces, erasing this necessity and so depriving us of this possibility. But project work requires us to integrate our puzzle piece with the puzzle pieces of others, who are equally confused. Because of this, projects unavoidably transform us into blind men arrayed around an elephant and leave us struggling to comprehend an ungraspable whole. Our situation encourages us to pursue coherence because our collective success depends upon our integrating orthogonal (meaning really different, even more different than we expected to find) perspectives. This integration is coherence.

The most successful projects always feature coherent experiences, where the participants walk through cognitive walls together. In this timeless state within our time-bound undertakings, our project's goals pale compared with our passionate pursuit of our purpose. Yet the literature focuses on helping us get better at setting and achieving goals, even though that never turns out to be the purpose behind the most successful projects. How curious.

Creating this book has been a series of naive beginnings punctuated with unsettling information. In this process, a true community has emerged around this elephant, and within that community has come the coherence we each always secretly aspire to experience.

I extend my grateful prayers for all the prayers unanswered in this pursuit. As with all writers, my original goal was immediate acceptance. I appreciate my friends, colleagues, and teachers who each cared enough to deprive me of this hollow success. They each in their own way demonstrated their deep caring for me and my work by overlaying their perspectives onto my unavoidably naive beginnings. A higher quality elephant has emerged for us as a result.

The list of contributors is long and impossible to properly appreciate here. I will rely upon the continuing coherence within our shared adventure to properly acknowledge their contributions. For the record, though, these are the principal contributors to this remarkable result.

The earliest reviewers reassured me that I was on the right track. I appreciate my wife and partner, Amy Schwab; my dear friend and teacher Naomi Karten; my brother, III; my folks, Bob and Bonnie Schmaltz; my sisters, Kathy Carey and Carol Smith; Martine Devos; Antoinette Hubbard; Rich Van Horn; and my partner and dear friend Mark G. Gray.

I appreciate my son, Wilder Schmaltz. You brought the elephant and the blind men to life with your extraordinary drawings.

I appreciate my past, present, and future clients who read later versions of the manuscript and provided unwanted but sorely needed insights along with their endorsing comments: Mark Lewis, Rick Gemereth, Walt Syzonenko, Edgar Zalite, Jim Goughnouer, Bill Burnett, and Chuck Kolsted. I appreciate those friends and associates who agreed to read and comment on the work: Jerry Weinberg for finding the first draft unreadable, David Socha for calling me at a nightclub in Minneapolis with searing questions, Dan Starr for the boat ride and the humor, Joshua Kerievsky for an unnameable something, David Wilczewski for challenging questions, James Bullock for opting out, Randy Taylor for the long conversations, and

Peter DeJager for considering the proposition; also Brad Reddersen, Brian Lassiter, and Susan Pecuch.

Special blind-men-arrayed-around-an-elephant appreciation for the manuscript reviewers, who read and commented at great and productive length: Thank you Don Yates, Dan Bieger, Irene Sitbon, Jeff Kulick, and Alis Valencia.

Thanks to my copy editor, Elissa Rabellino, for tolerating my feral grammar and making the parables sound right.

Thank you, Craig Neal, for connecting me with Berrett-Koehler, and thanks to the folks at Berrett-Koehler for engaging in the conversation, asking impossible questions, and dreaming big: Steven Piersanti, Jeevan Sivasubramaniam, Robin Donovan, Richard Wilson, and Michael Crowley.

And last but not least, my deep appreciation to Ivan Nahem for pointing out the Master/Slave relationship. It was right there but unacknowledged until you put a name on it.

David A. Schmaltz
Walla Walla, Washington
October 2002

THE BLIND MEN

THE BLIND MEN AND THE ELEPHANT

It was six men of Indostan
To learning much inclined,
Who went to see the Elephant
(Though all of them were blind),
That each by observation
Might satisfy his mind.

The First approached the Elephant,
And happening to fall
Against his broad and sturdy side,
At once began to bawl:
"God bless me! but the Elephant
Is very like a wall!"

The Second, feeling of the tusk,
Cried, "Ho! what have we here,
So very round and smooth and sharp?
To me 'tis mighty clear
This wonder of an Elephant
Is very like a spear!"

The Third approached the animal,
And happening to take
The squirming trunk within his hands,
Thus boldly up he spake:
"I see," quoth he, "the Elephant
Is very like a snake!"

The Fourth reached out an eager hand,
And felt about the knee:
"What most this wondrous beast is like
Is mighty plain," quoth he;
"'Tis clear enough the Elephant
Is very like a tree!"

The Fifth, who chanced to touch the ear,
Said: "E'en the blindest man
Can tell what this resembles most;
Deny the fact who can,
This marvel of an Elephant
Is very like a fan!"

The Sixth no sooner had begun
About the beast to grope,
Than, seizing on the swinging tail
That fell within his scope,
"I see," quoth he, "the Elephant
Is very like a rope!"

And so these men of Indostan
Disputed loud and long,
Each in his own opinion
Exceeding stiff and strong,
Though each was partly in the right,
And all were in the wrong!

Moral:
So oft in theologic wars,
The disputants, I ween,
Rail on in utter ignorance
Of what each other mean,
And prate about an Elephant
Not one of them has seen!

—John Godfrey Saxe (1816–1887)

CHALLENGING OUR CERTAINTY

A revolution in project work has exploded over the last decade. Companies now create products in radically different ways than before. Instead of dedicated teams mustered to achieve reasonable goals, cross-functional, highly technical, fast-time-to-market–driven teams are common. Product requirements have shifted away from a definite set toward an indefinable one. Not surprisingly, product-development teams now disappoint more often than they deliver. Many more projects fail to satisfy their sponsors' expectations than ever satisfy them.

Most project traditions persist in spite of these fundamental changes. Most companies expect project managers to control these projects the way they controlled simpler projects in the past.

- Management lays fixed track, expecting everyone to get on it and stay on it, or get back on it should they stray.
- Funding authorities cling to traditional success criteria, expecting "on-time, on-budget, on-spec" performance, in spite of this shifting context.
- Auditors continue to expect detailed plans early in projects, even though both auditors and project managers know they will be shocked by the magnitude of the changes in them over time.
- Managers still gauge progress by inches, expecting their team members to explain every deviation from the plotted course.

I speak with a certain client every few months. He's spearheading his organization's process-improvement effort. He reports his shortcomings each time we chat. His original plan targeted a broad set of changes. A few months later, his results forced him to reduce the scope. His fallback plan called for heavy customer involvement, which the customers couldn't deliver. He's frustrated with his obvious lack of progress. Every time we talk, he reports that he's working longer hours. "This place just doesn't get it," he says. "The status quo seems to be winning."

He has finally accomplished a significant toehold toward his objective, but he expected to be at the top of the cliff by now.

Rather than celebrating his significant breakthroughs, he punishes himself and those around him for an obvious "lack of progress." Of course the breakthroughs don't seem very significant when compared with what the original plan said was supposed to happen.

Some authors call these projects "wicked." I think this term misses the point. James Thurber told the story of his Civil War–veteran grandfather's relationship with the automobile. His grandpa thought of his car as just another sort of horse, and a particularly stupid and unmanageable horse at that. He never learned that the automobile would not turn when told to and that cars need different guidance techniques from what horses need. He died blaming the stupid car for his accidents. Calling these projects "wicked" duplicates Grandpa Thurber's error. Approach them inappropriately and they instantly become wicked.

I prefer the term *fuzzy*. "Wicked" sounds as if our automobile has something against us. "Fuzzy" sounds indistinct without suggesting any evil motive. Like Grandpa Thurber with his Hupmobile, we turn our otherwise innocently fuzzy projects into wicked ones. Our traditions, like Grandpa Thurber's, seem the source of what we experience as wicked:

- We create maps without surveying the territory.
- We follow these maps as if they were based upon knowledge rather than belief.
- We oblige others to follow these imaginary maps, as if following imaginary maps were reasonable.
- We promise rewards if targets are reached, as if any individual controlled the imaginary maps' accuracy.
- We threaten to punish those who miss targets, as if missing targets meant that someone had a personal problem or a professional shortcoming.

Our promises and threats justify a remarkable variety of inhuman acts:

- Requiring "voluntary" sacrifices as if they demonstrate sincere commitment.
- Demanding obedience as if that demonstrates dedication.

- Suspecting others as if that demonstrates prudence.
- Coercing as if that could encourage people to work together.
- Punishing as if that motivates.
- "Holding feet to the fire" as if that would entice action.

Misery results from these tactics more often than does project success. Until I started working in Silicon Valley, I had never met anyone making a quarter of a million dollars a year who felt taken mean advantage of by his or her employer. I've met several there.

We create the wickedness we experience as "wicked projects." We do this by interpreting our experiences in ways that not only undermine our success but guarantee meaninglessness. This simple acknowledgment transforms these experiences. I am never a powerless victim unless I abrogate my authority as the author of my own meaningless experiences. I have a guaranteed never-ending search for resolution as long as I believe that this wickedness originates somewhere else. Acknowledging myself as the source gives me the power to master these difficult experiences.

But mastering means losing some of the notions that helped me feel so powerful in the past. My convictions crumble as I accept that I cannot plan predictively enough to keep myself or anyone else safe from encountering unsettling information along the way. I can be confident only that our project will not turn out as planned. Incompetence no longer explains missed obligations, nor can I guarantee success by promising juicy payoffs. My certainties have to crumble, too. I cannot manage my project as if it were a manufacturing process. Deviations aren't necessarily bad. They can signal more meaningful success.

Our projects have shifted into a world where

- Personal sacrifice won't repel failure.
- Obedience can't attract success.
- Failure doesn't mean that anyone was untrustworthy.
- Coercion compromises capabilities.
- Punishments and enticements don't motivate.

If this shift seems scary to you, welcome to the club. It seems scary to me, too. I've concluded that shifting away from my confidence and my convictions *should* scare and confuse me. What experience could have prepared any of us for challenging our own certainties?

CONFUSING OURSELVES

I recently read a blurb about a new project management book. It promised to teach me how to act in order to make my projects successful. I thought, "Is this theater?" Perhaps it is.

Within that book's frame of reference, the project manager is the playwright, the casting director, and the acting coach. The project manager creates the script for the project. Then he acts as casting director, assigning roles and responsibilities. Then, switching roles again, he coaches his cast into following his script. The acting-coach project manager has a tool kit filled with techniques for compelling others to deliver predictable performances. He coaches by reasoning, persuading, or, if someone insists upon being unreasonable and contrary, by coercing. He assesses performance by observing behavior.

I've had my behavior "managed," just as I've managed others' behavior. Did I really force people to behave? I suppose I did. I created a plan, a script of obligations; then I held each actor's feet to the fire. Under these conditions, their contributions had all the juiciness of a mortgage payment. Each contribution became an obligation, when it could have been so much more. Why did I work so hard to create such mediocre results?

Most project managers bring this acting-coach frame of reference to their fuzzy projects. We might prefer something other than coercion, but what can replace this crumbling body of knowledge we call "project management"? Must we continue yelling at the steering wheel like Thurber's grandfather, unaware that we are the ones confusing ourselves when it doesn't respond?

CHOOSING MORE APPROPRIATE
FRAMES OF REFERENCE
· ·

Do we have to be in the behavior modification business to successfully manage projects? I have a devil of a time planning a project if I cannot predict how anyone will behave when working on it. I simplify planning if I can at least assume predictability. I can track and control more easily if everyone stays within my prescribed boundaries. But the fuzziness, the indistinctness, makes such predictions unlikely.

Methodologies attempt to shave this fuzziness from fuzzy projects by offering templates designed to make the indistinct more definite. Most work-breakdown structures must have been designed by the compulsive progeny of Frederick Winslow Taylor, the self-proclaimed father of scientific management. Taylor believed that each manager was the benevolent father of his workers; that the manager's proper role was to allocate work according to skills and to assign workers as required by the work, while limiting the opportunities for what Taylor called "soldiering"—what we might call "unplanned interaction." What passed for science when Taylor claimed his fatherhood doesn't pass for science anymore. Science advanced a century while Taylor and his now-pseudoscientific followers stood still.

Much of what we call "project management" stands upon Taylor's flat-earth perspectives. When applied to repeatable manufacturing situations, his primitive notions have great utility. The same ideas fall apart when applied in more human, less mechanical contexts. Success requires something other than simply shaving a project's fuzziness. Our well-intended barbering leaves us bound with unanswerable questions. We might want efficient projects, but how do we improve the efficiency of a single-instance project when efficiency can only be meaningfully considered as a function of many similar instances? We might want a good plan, but how can we create an effective script for a discovery when we cannot know at the start what we'll discover or how we'll discover it?

Our centuries-long struggle to predict our futures has come to this; innocent attempts to manage our futures create unmanageable ones, well-intended efforts to script the play undermine the purpose of the performance. Our directing guarantees mediocrity. We've filled our kit with tools we're much better off not using. Our traditions mislead us into using them anyway.

The unpredictability—the indistinctness of today's efforts—had better not be a problem, because this fuzziness has become an unavoidable feature of our present and future projects. Our projects' fuzziness ranks as no more (or less) of a problem than Grandpa Thurber's inability to tell his car to turn. Just like Grandpa Thurber's, our interpretations transform a benign feature into an unresolvable shortcoming. Grandpa Thurber's car was no more like a horse than our present projects are like past ones. It was as unreasonable for Grandpa Thurber to expect his car to behave like a horse as it is for us to expect ancient tactics to guide today's projects. Just like many project managers today, the old man created his own troubles by innocently overextending his frame of reference.

We each place our experiences inside such frames of reference, or *frames*. These frames subtly influence what we believe and how we behave. For instance, some people put driving a car into a "driving a race car" frame and so justify as appropriate a different set of behaviors from those of someone who puts driving into a "'chauffeur'" frame. We are usually unaware of these frames' influence on us. We might not even experience making a choice as we step into another one.

The word *project* can push me unawares into a playwright/casting-director/acting-coach frame, in which I, as the project manager, automatically begin writing the script, selecting the cast, and coaching the performers. I'm both enabled and trapped by this frame. I'm enabled because a whole set of behaviors automatically kicks in whenever I employ this frame. I'm also trapped because another set of behaviors automatically evaporates. My choices are limited by whatever frame I choose (or whatever frame chooses me), so it's important that I choose appropriate frames. When I am unaware that I've chosen my frame, I am left, like Thurber's grandfather, missing opportunities to improve my own situation. I yell at a lot of steering wheels.

What frames might I choose for project work? Our traditions position my choices of reference frames along a continuum, ranging from authority to anarchy. As a project manager, I usually equated the degree of personal control with the likelihood of success, as if my participation guaranteed collective success. Can you hear Taylor's ghost rattling his compulsive chains?

There must be an infinite number of frames to choose from when considering project work. Some of the most popular project manager frames hold project managers to be

- Fathers, where they coach and punish
- Mothers, where they nurture and instruct
- Magicians, where they pull rabbits out of hats
- Zookeepers, where they keep the wild animals well fed in cages
- Priests, where they exhort and forgive
- Comedians, where they entertain
- Teachers, where they instruct and grade
- Lobbyists, where they influence the support of the powerful
- Sheep, where they follow others' orders
- Wolves, where they take advantage of sheep
- Omniscient beings, where they know and see all (or are supposed to)
- Village idiots, where they get it wrong no matter what they try to do

Each frame brings with it a set of frame-appropriate behaviors and a set of frame-inappropriate behaviors. What frame do you find yourself in when you participate in project work?

How would your present project be different if you looked at it from within a "projects are conversations between peers" frame? Such conversations are never scripted. The conversation's potential diminishes when one conversant controls the other's responses. Why even engage if you know how the conversation will turn out? How are conversations controlled? No one centrally controls them, yet anarchy does not usually define the outcome. Conversations are dances that literally find their own way, based upon the judgment and skill of the dancers. Skilled dancers' steps quite naturally integrate when the dancers hear the same music. Culture influences. Intent colors. No one decides how conversations conclude.

Most project wickedness starts because it seems appropriate at the time. I'm assigned a project. I unconsciously slip into my playwright/casting-director/acting-coach frame. I plan the effort. I bring my schedule to you and entice you into engaging in the effort. I monitor your steps, keeping you on track by frequently reminding you of your promises and the payoff. You respond enthusiastically at first, but over time the obligation leaves you shuffling through deepening meaninglessness. I engage in a series of acting-coach, behavior modification activities, intended to get you "back on track." We both know it will be your fault if you fail to deliver. We both eventually understand that you cannot help but fail under the terms we've brought to the effort.

The *leader* and *follower* frames influence most projects today. Where appropriate, where the leaders can know enough to know where they are going and how to get there, where someone's simple compliance can guarantee success, these frames might be appropriate windows onto the world. Where these conditions do not exist, leader and follower metaphors fall apart. If no one knows, who should write the script? If the leader can't know, whom should the followers follow? In these circumstances, staying within these frames limits the questions we ask and the solutions we consider, encouraging a tenacious meaninglessness.

Putting a fuzzy effort into a leader/follower frame can justify no end of wickedness. A typical bout of such wickedness sounds like this: "You are required to estimate the unknowable and then commit to these projections so that you can be rewarded based upon your delivery." You know you have only random influence over the outcome. How could this not become a meaningless frame?

Changing the frame can change everything. If I want to change my behavior, I'm best able to do it not by laboriously changing my behaviors (that's hard) but by changing the frame within which these behaviors seem appropriate (this can be easy). I create the potential for everything else to change when I shift my interpretation of my experience. After my seven-year-old son came home from school and said, "Daddy, my teacher said that smoking kills people. Are you trying to kill yourself?" I couldn't continue thinking about smoking in the same way. I still had the habit, but rather than satisfying me, it unsettled me. I quit smoking within six months.

I could imagine no other way within this new frame to resolve the contradiction of a pleasurable experience that unsettled me.

Neither you nor I can operate without frames; no one can. And while we might not be aware of the frame surrounding us, some frame must always be there. These windows make our experiences meaningful. We cannot do away with frames, but we can become more aware of the frames we employ and choose to employ more personally meaningful ones.

The search for a more meaningful way of coping with our fuzzy responsibilities might not require anything more than choosing a different frame of reference, and only we can be in charge of making this choice. Changing our behaviors seems doomed to fail. Increasing our leaders' authority seems beside the point—just so much yelling into the steering wheel. If we can find more appropriate frames of reference, new sets of more steering wheel–appropriate behaviors might quite naturally emerge. We might even find ourselves using our steering wheels for steering.

A DIFFERENT SET OF POSSIBILITIES

What frame might be more appropriate for coping with our fuzzy responsibilities?

I like the "Blind Men and the Elephant" frame. For me, it perfectly captures the spirit of these undertakings. I suppose John Godfrey Saxe could have had no idea of the power that his simple poem could bring to those of us trying to pull meaningful results out of fuzzy projects. He chooses six blind men to examine an elephant that none can see. Each discovers something unique. Their discoveries perfectly match the key dilemmas facing all of us who are blindly pursuing our own meaningful results:

- One blind man interprets the side of the elephant as being the wall between himself and anything meaningful.
- Another blind man interprets the elephant's tusk as being the spear that a good soldier might feel obligated to carry into battle.

- Yet another blind man interprets the trunk as being the snake that no one should trust.
- Still another blind man interprets the elephant's leg as being the tree trunk supporting his efforts.
- Another blind man interprets the elephant's ear as being the fan that he might use to coax an ember into a flame.
- And the last blind man interprets the elephant's tail as being the rope that can tie together a coherent whole.

Our wickedest projects feature much of what Saxe characterizes as "rail[ing] on in utter ignorance of what each other mean." These arguments illustrate the most common fuzzy-project problem, incoherence—the inability of blind men to create common interpretation from their shared experience. Their differing frames of reference and their "utter ignorance" of each other's frames create their encumbering incoherence.

The incoherence that comes from employing inappropriate frames of reference creates the wickedness that victimizes us so. How different might their experiences be if each blind man could embrace every other blind man's different and disturbing testimony? They don't have to share the same frame if they can accept and integrate each other's stories about their unique frames. No meaningful elephant appears for the blind men without this simple but elusive capacity. If each cannot share this understanding, their interactions spawn no more than the same complications found in their "theologic wars" we call wicked projects.

What happens to our actor and director roles within the "Blind Men and the Elephant" frame? A predictable wickedness results if one of the blind men has more authority than the others and becomes stuck within the director frame. This director can inadvertently destroy collective meaning by insisting that everyone describe his or her elephant piece as being very much like his "fan." Another sort of wickedness results when one of the blind men becomes stuck within an actor frame and, because he doesn't want to appear insubordinate, reports that his elephant leg seems like a fan. Incoherence reigns in both situations. No elephant emerges.

Each of us blind men shares the same dilemma: How might we transform our project's fuzziness into coherent, collectively meaningful results? In the following chapters I describe how shifting my frames of reference has transformed my project work's fuzziness into more meaningful results, even when those around me were unable or chose not to shift their frames. We are each a marvel of adaptive ability, but we unnecessarily hobble ourselves whenever we unconsciously adopt inappropriately limiting frames of reference. I hope this book will help you become more aware of the frames you use, improve your ability to choose more meaningful frames for yourself, and help you to help others find more useful frames for their parts of your common experience.

In the following chapters, I will introduce you to this elephant of meaningful coherence and to each of the blind men's perspectives, embracing in turn their wall, their spear, their snake, their tree, their fan, and their rope. May you find here more meaningful possibilities than you've found within frames of reference you've used in the past.

THE ELEPHANT

It was six men of Indostan
To learning much inclined,
Who went to see the Elephant
(Though all of them were blind),
That each by observation
Might satisfy his mind.

—From "The Blind Men and the
Elephant," by John Godfrey Saxe

AN ELEPHANT WE CANNOT SEE

Each project engagement reminds me again of these blind men around an elephant. Each blind man discovers a piece of an overall ungraspable whole. From within each individual's personal experience, it seems only reasonable to conclude that everyone else arrayed around the beast experiences this animal as he does, that his personal experience reasonably mirrors every other's, but it most certainly does not. When each blind man can integrate with his own perspective every other blind man's curious testimony, a collective coherence emerges along with the elephant. This coherence creates remarkable possibilities, as if the blind men could actually see through each other's eyes. When they cannot integrate their stories, as John Godfrey Saxe reminds us, their projects degrade into the incoherence of "theologic wars," where each combatant endlessly argues against every other combatant's religiously held opinion. Such deeply held differences of opinion cannot be logically resolved. These wars are won only by those refusing to engage in battle.

Such battles didn't always bore me as they do today. When I ferociously argued that my meanings should dominate on my projects, my clever arguments seemed certain to settle something. Instead, my impassioned opinions at best narrowed necessary diversity, resonating only the perspective of one refusing to acknowledge his own blindness. Those engaging as I did never notice that winning these arguments loses the wars.

My pivotal moment came as I caught myself being myself. After years of believing that I was my projects' meaning-maker, I quite by accident experienced what it was like for those working for me. My delusion collapsed as I caught myself insisting that others' experiences were wrong so that I could maintain my own narrow toehold on reality. Those holding opposing perspectives, whom I'd pushed out in favor of my "superior perspective," didn't return when I needed them. I was in this moment of extremity left with only my irrelevant elephant part while "my" team abandoned me and my so-called leadership.

What is coherence, this magical property, this elephant we cannot see? Leadership in this blind-men-and-elephant world requires integrating disparate perspectives, not enforcing a dominant one. Our projects are poorly served by the belief, religiously defended, that leaders create meaning for their team, because they can at best only encourage some preconditions that might provoke an emerging coherence of shared meaning; acknowledging their own, personal blindness is the most prominent among these. The ability of the many blind men arrayed around the elephant to integrate their personal meanings into a shared experience really creates coherence. Acknowledged blind men create such coherence. If they believed they could see, what would possibly encourage them to work so meaningfully together?

How might we make our project work delight each other? Our hierarchies smother understanding. Our work breakdowns simply break down. Dominion doesn't listen. Compromise can't comprehend. Coherence has never been the sole property of any leader. The coherence we crave, this elephant our projects so desperately require, has always been within the grasp of everyone on every project. Like the image of the elephant, coherence emerges easily from within some frames of reference and suffocates in others. Like the blind men in Saxe's poem, we can always destroy our own possibilities for coherence by insisting that we know all about this elephant that not one of us will ever see. Unlike Saxe's blind men, we can create coherence by losing some of our unwarranted certainty.

MASTERS AND SLAVES

February 2, 2002, 10 a.m.
Lower Manhattan, New York

The whole commerce between master and slave is a perpetual exercise of the most boisterous passions, the most unremitting despotism on the one part, and degrading submission on the other.
—Thomas Jefferson

We have arranged the training-room tables into four rectangles—each with five chairs, two on two sides and one on the end—facing the front of the room. In the back and on the north side, windows overlook the street, where, interspersed with detoured taxis, buses, and cars, a constant stream of trucks carry debris from the remains of the nearby World Trade Center. The background traffic noise leaves us straining to hear each other.

A project management workshop started an hour before, and progress has already slowed. The walls are papered with half-completed lists of difficulties, and these glower down like gargoyles over twenty pairs of slackening shoulders as the reality of our project work lives settles over us. A darkening drizzle of rain starts outside, and the room feels uncomfortably warm. Time crawls.

We are considering difficulties, when one student stands, looks at those sitting around a table across the room, and with a gleam in his eye declares, "The problem with you is that you do not properly appreciate the Master-Slave relationship."

No one shows any sign of surprise, shock, or indignation. A moment of silence introduces a twittering instead, as if he has expressed a universally recognized but unspeakable truth.

His comment was a joke, of course. But like all excellent humor, it contained a painfully large portion of truth.

Consider the working relationships on your projects today. One customer confided that when she first started working at her company, her mentor suggested, "If anything goes seriously wrong, just blame the project." Projects and their constituencies have always had complicated relationships. Ask about these complications and you'll find no disagreement between any constituency's description of the tangles. Everyone knows the open secret—their customers hold them in considerable contempt. We unconsciously re-create Jefferson's famous insight, a summary of which still looks down on visitors to his memorial in Washington, D.C.: "Commerce between master and slave is despotism."

Few properly appreciate this Master-Slave relationship.

We hold these truths to be self-evident and immutable: Someone's supposed to be responsible for telling someone else what to do; others are responsible for taking orders. The Masters and the Slaves seem to select themselves for their roles without considering the terrible consequences of their innocent choices. One becomes the despot, while another becomes that person's Slave. Does project work have to be organized this way?

FRAGMENTING ALONG PREDICTABLE LINES

One director-level project manager tells the story of her first visit to her project's unheated customer site on a cold winter Saturday. When she arrived clad in boots and a heavy coat to begin work, which involved some complicated system testing, her customer counterpart informed her, "Project people are not allowed to use customer chairs."

Thinking this was a joke, she took a seat, knowing that executing six hours' worth of exacting tests would only be complicated by completing the work while standing, but this requirement was no joke. She stood for six hours, shivering while testing on an unheated shop floor.

The customer often plays the role of despot to his project's Slave. On a first client visit, I chatted in an elevator with three people heading to their project sponsor's status meeting. They confided that they were going to actively withhold critical project information during the meeting. Why deceive? Disclosing their project's real situation would have just encouraged their sponsor's smothering involvement. The project folks knew that if they didn't shave the truth, they couldn't succeed. More important, they knew that if they didn't withhold some facts, their customer couldn't succeed, either.

Such pressures to succeed create overly responsible Slaves and irresponsible Masters. Every Slave sometimes subverts his Master's orders, not simply so he can survive as a Slave, but so his Master can come close to achieving her objectives. The alternatives all look worse. Failing to deliver brings the Master's punishment. Fully disclosing problems implies the Slave's incompetence in every reported complication. Full disclosure invites the Master's disruptive intrusion or destructive punishment, neither of which improves anyone's possibilities for success.

Every Master knows the feeling of having herself cast as a Slave by her customers, too. Each customer, in turn, encourages a Slave-like relationship on his downstream providers, rendering each a Slave unable to say no and unwittingly leaving each therefore also unable to offer a responsible yes. Whenever no becomes unspeakable, every remaining yes becomes worthless. This dynamic recreates a tragedy as each "Master" insists upon satisfaction from her "Slaves" without regard to the effects on other constituencies. When each Slave becomes responsible for delivering to impossibly irrational demands, each in turn finds his own opportunities to assume the role of Master-for-a-moment, passing these insidious expectations throughout his projects. Since real-world results must eventually resolve this irrationality into something tangible, this downwardly passed buck inevitably stops in the lap of the Slave lowest in the pecking order, who must resolve his orders, no matter how irrational, into some working result. Or not.

Resolving this absurd chain becomes unendingly contentious, punctuated with derisive whisperings or outright uprisings as each constituency complains of his own powerlessness in the face of his Master's unending despotism. Inject a reward system that either randomly favors or encourages personal contribution over collective effort, and it's a wonder that anyone ever accomplishes anything with anyone else. Furthermore, many organizations operate under a "Chinese Wall" ethic, dictating that information be shared only on a presumed-need-to-know basis, framing full disclosure as a bad thing. All of these contextual conditions work very effectively to undermine most possibilities for meaningful improvement. More significantly, they create a climate in which failure can be reasonably assumed from the outset.

Organizations operating under such pressures fragment along predictable lines. Where despotism prevails,

- "Us" and "them" crowd out "we."
- Rules disqualify individual judgment.
- Public secrets and private subversions proliferate.
- The truth becomes unspeakable.

We inflict these results on ourselves, although we might never catch ourselves in the act of inflicting. Our traditions mislead us into inappropriate roles and unfulfillable responsibilities just as if they were reasonable expectations.

DISCLOSING OUR DELUSION

Failure is not an option.

— Homily seen on a manager's wall

If failure is not an option, it becomes an imperative. Under the terms of the Master-Slave relationship, failure becomes unavoidable and the fault of whomever was assigned the lowest "responsible" Slave position in the pecking order. Most projects don't begin fearing failure, they start by denying the inevitability of it. There are only so many times anyone can begin hopefully under these conditions before hopefulness becomes naïveté. A sense of hopelessness displaces natural optimism. Individuals wisely hunker down for another ordeal rather than standing up anticipating a fresh opportunity. This hunkering down looks like cynicism, but thoughtful reasoning really supports it. The continuing ordeal wears people down.

In this context, more detailed rules, policy statements, and procedure definitions just more finely delineate ancient battle lines. Assigned authority might transform Slaves into temporary Masters, but only at the cost of making themselves substitute Slaves. Whoever is cast in the Master's role might get to have her say but not exactly her way. Masters become no more powerful than Slaves within this inexorable, exhausting, and seemingly unending swirl. Rationalizing work processes under these conditions becomes absurdity. Why improve your ability to estimate how much "stuff" will fit into a ten-pound sack when the Master says that fifteen pounds must fit into it and you cannot say no? Why insist that an objective be met in the next quarter when some expert will just insist that your goal cannot be met?

Paradox creeps in. People respond to such crazy-making conditions by acting crazy. In fact, crazy passes as sane on such projects. We unconsciously engage in the classic paradoxical tactics that thrive under Master-Slave relationships.

1. We force spontaneity by demanding that Slaves "just do it," resolving conflicts by encouraging them to proceed as if they could succeed without careful consideration, when "just doing it" can't help but prompt meaningless pursuit.

2. We avoid inevitabilities by attempting to wait Masters out, working as if unworkable plans could succeed when we feel powerless to change them, when unworkable plans simply encourage meaningless work.

3. We require behaviors rather than results, turning both Slaves and Masters into idiots with our less-than-generous interpretations, when ignoring the meanings we make of our behavior guarantees that we can only have collectively meaningless interactions.

4. We require voluntary compliance, stealing choices by insisting that Slaves cannot say no, when refusing to take no for an answer renders any resulting yes meaningless.

5. We engage in endless finger-pointing "did not, did too" controversies, interpreting escalating denial as further evidence of guilt, when if we have no doubt, we cannot give anyone, including ourselves, the benefit of it.

Such despotism discloses only delusion.

LIBERATING OURSELVES

Most nurse notions that someone else should be able to change this insanity:

"If only the customers would make more reasonable demands."

"If only the executives would assert themselves and say no!"

"If only the project would produce accurate estimates and deliver on its commitments."

Master-Slave relationships stick here. *Our Masters include anyone whom we believe has the power to change such difficulties. The Slaves are those we believe do not hold such power.*

As a rule, customers don't make rational demands, executives don't tell customers no, and no one has ever, except by accident, produced accurate estimates for novel undertakings or reliably delivered on coerced commitments. Not yet in this universe.

If there has never been a leverage point in making customers rational, making executives empathetic, or improving estimation and delivery, what are the real points of leverage in our project work? Over the last decade, I have been teaching unconventional "project management" workshops intended to help people discover points of leverage that effectively co-opt their Master-Slave relationships. I'm writing this book to introduce, demonstrate, and properly explain these leverage points because without them, projects seem to endlessly pursue imperatives that cannot make any difference in either the quality of anyone's experience or the effectiveness of a project's results. Without these leverage points, project work becomes a meaningless, cruel game without end.

These leverage points are reminders. They more often awaken a slumbering understanding than create any new ones. Being reminded of something I've forgotten usually upsets me, especially if the reminder isn't particularly profound, and these leverage points seem anything but profound. They seem useless in the face of my real-world difficulties, but being reminded should upset those of us who have unwittingly taken it upon ourselves to become more demanding Masters, more perfect Slaves, or more hopeful Don Quixotes.

These leverage points are:

- Purpose as an antidote to difficulty
- Generosity in the face of uncertainty
- Personal judgment to counteract meaninglessness
- Patience to neutralize chaos
- Acknowledging our own blindness to encourage coherence

Exercising these leverage points should feel unsafe, because exercising them *is* unsafe, but then the Master-Slave relationship is unsafe, too—unsafe but familiar. Because each of these points violates some part of every Master-Slave relationship, we must deploy them stealthily. If the Master ever got wind that responsibility was being shared or imperatives ignored, she might, like a furious grade-school teacher, punish the perpetrators. Or so the story goes. Such un-Slave-like behavior mostly succeeds, but so few attempt it that almost no one knows that it does. Most important, it returns to the former Slave his latitude for action. Masters are almost always less diligent than they threaten to be, with far fewer teeth than anyone expected. In fact, when the Slaves begin actively co-opting their Master-Slave relationships, their Masters become liberated, too.

Acknowledging that we create the Masters and the Slaves in our lives can seem improbable from within the Slave's role. That the Slave has the most power in these relationships seems completely unlikely. The balance of this book considers awakening this nascent understanding and deciding to do something about it.

I am fomenting a quiet revolution here, one that acknowledges our true sources of power and encourages each participant to accept his proper responsibility for the meaningfulness of his experiences. The Masters in our lives are hopeless creatures, unable to satisfy the expectations we unintentionally pass on to them and they just as innocently and self-destructively embrace. The Slaves in our lives live just as meaninglessly, eventually tumbling to the inexorable conclusion that their Masters are heartless or powerless rather than just as clueless as they have been. It doesn't have to be this way.

I have over the past decade been challenging my clients' misattributions—whom they call Master and whom they call Slave. In this time, and in my earlier careers, I've seen more ineptness than evil, more ignorance than intention, and much more unwarranted certainty than enlightened understanding. The real enemy becomes the certainty that comes from thinking one knows what no one could possibly know about another—that phony vision a blind man might proclaim, which fools no one but the blind man.

But refusing to engage in battle doesn't mean sitting idly beneath any "Master's" thumb. We each ultimately sit only under our own thumbs, anyway. People want safety, but insisting upon safety before acting ensures only sitting, not acting (or safety). There are no Masters or Slaves, only our illusions of Masters and Slaves.

"THAT EACH BY OBSERVATION MIGHT SATISFY HIS MIND"

My job here will never be more than to remind you of what you always suspected and probably half-knew. If we cannot engage with each other as peers, as adults, as Master to Master, we each become Slave to a thoroughly disempowering hierarchical idea, one as old and as wrong as the divine right of kings. The organization that issues your paycheck is not your Master or you its Slave. You have all of the power and authority you need, in your present position, to liberate yourself from your Master-Slave relationships. You can make the difference that will make a difference in your project experience, even if no one else changes. If this seems unlikely, observe and satisfy your own mind.

Master-Slave relationships stand between us and coherence, the elephant that emerges whenever we are engaging in our most effective project work. Yet we carry on as if this resident inconvenience were not inconveniencing us. We mostly don't discuss it. We giggle when someone stands and complains that others do not properly appreciate it. We hunker down and engage as if it weren't there, even though our experience should have shown us the foolishness in this behavior. We step gingerly, carrying on as if we were not disgusted by the smell and encumbered by the detours. We might live better without these relationships, but can we imagine our lives without this encumbrance?

This book imagines a life acknowledging rather than continually accommodating the Master-Slave relationships among us. I will poke at how you engage in project work and suggest some alternatives. I will feel comfortable assuming that you are the most powerful project management tool you will ever use, and I will demonstrate how you might choose to deploy this most powerful tool. You will not be alone in this conversation. I will also tell stories about how my certainties were poked and relate how I learned how to discover my own meaningful results within each of my project assignments. I will not suggest any massive organizational-change efforts because these, like most of the projects initiated in the world today, simply do not work. I will report, however, what has worked for me and for hundreds of people attending my Mastering Projects Workshop.

No one can mandate another's liberation. Dissolving a Master-Slave relationship's insidious chains requires free choice and personal initiative. (No one can demand that you take personal initiative without robbing you of it. I can only suggest that you consider this option.)

Expect your observations to surprise you. You might discover that you are, indeed, powerful enough in your present position to transform your project experiences into something other than endless tiptoeing around an apparently intractable relationship, even if no one else ever suspects.

Outside that training room's windows, down at street level in the Wall Street neighborhood bordering the World Trade Center's destruction, notions of Master and Slave wrestle. Within those windows the same contest continues.

THE WALL

The First approached the Elephant,

And happening to fall

Against his broad and sturdy side,

At once began to bawl:

"God bless me! but the Elephant

Is very like a wall!"

—From "The Blind Men and the
Elephant," by John Godfrey Saxe

FESTINA LENTE—HASTEN SLOWLY

There's always someone at the start of every project. Someone's not ready, while everyone else strains at the reins. When we set to work, this one drags his feet. He complains about irrelevant things and seems not to be hastening slowly or otherwise. He's a pain in the butt.

Most ignore him and get on with their real work. Some try to push him off his dime. Sometimes they succeed in getting him moving with the others, but he engages hesitantly, as if he has left something important behind. Later he will seem to have forgotten about whatever felt so very important at the beginning, but the memory of it will occasionally return to inconvenience him, and his reaction then will inconvenience those around him.

We might be taught to hasten slowly at the beginning, to cautiously consider before proceeding, but most of us quickly figure out how to ditch any roadblock between us and full speed ahead, leaving the careful considerer behind. We take a deft sidestep or an innocent about-face, but we usually avoid the wall that so evidently blocks progress.

A wall marks the start of every project. Pay close attention, look carefully, or you'll miss it. After you've seen it, you might wish you could make it disappear. This wall can become a useful feature of your project, but it always first appears as an inconveniencing barrier to meaningful progress.

We are taught to hasten slowly for one very good reason—not to encumber progress, but to acknowledge and address one insignificant-seeming issue that later might seem anything but insignificant. We are not simply milling around as we struggle to make our first steps more deliberate, we are making our purpose explicit. Without an explicit purpose, project work tends to shift from raging enthusiasm into utter meaningless. Projects make this shift so imperceptibly and so inexorably that we are utterly disabled from slowing down to discover our purpose once we achieve full momentum. We will have one devil of a time recapturing that moment should we manage to hasten quickly through it.

The first time I encountered this wall, I sidestepped it and thought I was getting away with something. The second time I didn't even see it. I spent many years looking right through these walls just as if they were never there. It took another, wiser person to reacquaint me with my inconvenience. I have no end of gratitude for this introduction.

Where should a project start? Some say projects should start by gathering requirements. Others argue for setting objectives. Still others want boundaries defined. Most are satisfied just to get working on something, anything. Regardless of where they are supposed to start, projects start where they start. Most begin by initiating activity that will add no lasting value to anything, just so they can get moving.

Our training tells us to hasten slowly at the beginning. But something insidious happens to all who hasten. Hastening at the beginning will tempt us to try to avoid the initiating wall. And no one successfully avoids this wall.

Responding to an urgency by hastening creates the key failure mode for projects. Hastening makes us forget something that's essential for meaningful success. We'll discover what we've overlooked during our project's darkest days, when we can't get a break. When our approach betrays us and our objectives become absolutely unachievable, our wall will reappear. If we avoided it at the beginning, this wall will stop us cold then.

MEETING MY WALL (AGAIN)

I reported for my first day's work as a consultant ten years ago. A small training and consulting company had hired me away from a secure job in a large insurance company. I didn't know I was about to meet my wall.

I carefully prepared for that first morning of my new life. Up at 4 a.m., I worked out in both the gym and the pool. I ate a large breakfast. I chose a dark blue blazer to wear over a heavily starched light blue oxford cloth shirt. I decided against wearing the tie that I wouldn't have dared arriving without at my old job, and felt half-naked and a little decadent. I left the hotel an hour early, arriving at the office long before the office manager would show up to unlock the door. I must have looked anything but suitably clad in my polished penny loafers as I nervously paced the quarter block on either side of that suburban Silicon Valley office building. I was scared spitless and swooning with anticipation.

How could my background have landed me in this place? My résumé was nothing to write home about. I was not a scholar or a member of a prestigious society. My interview two weeks earlier had gone well. Each partner took time to share his or her stories. I showed well. A partner meeting, where I was an agenda item, ran into dinner, at which they asked me to join the firm. I accepted (details like salary and responsibilities to be fleshed out later) before slipping out of the restaurant and catching the last plane north for my final two weeks at the insurance company.

Observing was my primary qualification for this job. In my most desperate moments working at the insurance company, when abandoning my career as a songwriter and "getting a real job" seemed to have been an act of self-destruction, I found myself writing. I wrote about what I observed on my projects. I even wrote about the litter I passed on my walk to work. I used these observations, whatever they were, as a means of expressing myself. My powers of observation have always been a part of my life. They first led me to become a songwriter. Now my observing, rather than my knowing, had qualified me for this opportunity.

I had first connected with this consulting firm just before Thanksgiving the year before, when I audited the firm's project management workshop with the idea of bringing it into the insurance company for my staff of project managers. The trainer and I discovered a deep connection between us during the class, where we caught ourselves finishing each other's sentences, and as I left the workshop, I asked her if she would be interested in reviewing some of my writing. She was interested, and just after Christmas, having finished her review, she invited me down for an interview with the other partners. Now, the last week of the following February, I was coming on board and anxious to prove myself.

I'll never forget that early half-hour of pacing around the office. The California air was unseasonably warm for a guy used to Oregon Februarys. The sun felt moist and hot through the light haze. Alien-looking lilies bloomed from beds of creeping jasmine. Larry Howard, a founder of the firm, had volunteered to show me the ropes. His arrival interrupted my pacing. He proposed breakfast. We small-talked our way a short couple of blocks to a little café. He ordered an enormous meal, and as my earlier breakfast weighed heavily, I ordered an English muffin and some dishwater decaf.

Our conversation remained small throughout the meal. Then, as Larry swept up an errant bit of egg yolk with his last toast point, we finally began talking about where I would start.

I asked, "So, Larry, what do you want me to do today?"

Larry looked up at me with the slightest smile in one corner of his mouth. "That's not the right question. We don't do business like that," he replied. The look in my eyes caused a deeper glee to erupt on Larry's face. "Yes," he continued, "there's a more important question than what I or the firm wants you to do. Listen carefully," he said, his voice dropping to a conspiratorial whisper, "this is the essential question for you this morning. The question is, 'What do you want?'"

Larry was introducing me to my wall. I'm sure I looked stunned by his question. I felt dizzy. I felt trapped. I slipped into an embarrassed, mind-racing verbal tap dance. "What do I ... want?" I repeated Larry's question as if I hadn't heard or completely understood it.

"Yes," he repeated, "what is it that *you* want?"

Mistaking Larry for my Master and unconsciously shifting into my well-practiced Slave vocabulary, I slipped in a few of the loftier-sounding objectives from my last performance appraisal at the insurance company, but Larry would have none of my content-free bureaucratese.

He deftly countered, remaining powerful behind the shield of his damned question. "So, what did you say that you want?"

I listed the usual requirements, but they sounded strangely flat drifting across that breakfast table. I explained that I wanted to learn how to consult in high-technology companies. I would like to teach. I wanted to write a book. None of these comments satisfied Larry. He insisted that I become clear about my purpose for being in the firm. I would use the job as a medium, not as an end in itself, he explained, or there would be no work for me. I had to answer his question before he would assign me any meaningful responsibilities.

I could feel the air leaking out of the brightly colored aspiration that had lifted me out of the confining insurance company and into this job's seemingly unlimited potential. The initiation here was rough! Less than an hour into my employment and I already had to know what I wanted? I had to be clear about my personal priorities? I had to share these priorities with my partners? Larry was telling me that I'd have to get and stay real if I was going to succeed there. Gulp! I wanted this wall to disappear. I wanted my life to become simple again, like it had been just an hour before.

The idea of disclosing what I wanted terrified me after so many years of hiding in my Slave role at the insurance company. There, I was supposed to just get behind whatever assignment my Masters gave me. They encouraged self-sacrifice. I could have my own private purpose, but I had learned better than to share this with too many others. Sharing would give them ammunition for some future assault. I remember keeping my personal secrets for many years. I barely remember deciding that I'd be better off just forgetting any wider purpose. I finally buckled under and just did my work.

Larry could see the sparking and smoking behind my eyes, and he helped me a little bit, but only a little bit. (Larry was not about to save me from this most crucial lesson.) "I'll help," he promised. "We're here to support each other."

I felt rattled for the rest of the day. My mind continued to sort through possibilities in the shadow beneath this newly looming wall. While I sorted, Larry gave me a tour of the operation. He took me along on a consulting visit that afternoon, and he asked me to observe a meeting with a client. Afterward, my blunt and colorful assessment amused him. I felt my mind settling. I watched and reported, and engaged unself-consciously for a while, forgetting about the wall for the first time since breakfast. But Larry's question continued to poke like a thorn through my sock. What *did* I want? What did I *want*?

I did not elegantly enter that firm. The wall stalled me for weeks before I settled on a statement of what I really wanted. My discovery took me on a much longer and more difficult journey than even Larry could have predicted, and he had initiated several journeys before mine. I would never have believed him if he had told me how long my discovery would take. Years later, when that morning was a fading memory, a client helped me assign a proper name to my answer to Larry's question.

WITNESS

I always offer one-on-one consulting when I'm teaching a workshop. The real issues some people come to work on are unmentionable in public. Others, many others, need a listening ear or a sympathetic forehead from which to bounce their issues back at them. I'm more than happy to provide this service.

Sometimes I am sworn to secrecy. Several people have whispered to me tales of brutality that could not be discussed among their work groups. I referred one to counseling. Some of the people who sought my confidential advice left their jobs shortly after our conversation. Some reported later that something changed for them during our talk.

I take no special credit for any changes that occur. I well understand the power in simply talking about the unmentionable. People usually need to hear their own voice telling their own story to discover the opportunities hidden there. I know that if I can attend to their story, most will uncover their own transforming idea. Listening remains one of the least acknowledged consulting skills.

Last year I was teaching a workshop, and my off-teaching times were booked up as usual. I expected a series of empathic chats, but one conversation surprised me. A young woman asked me to lunch to "talk." This could mean anything. It's her agenda, I remember thinking as I noted the day and time.

We ordered and began the usual small talk.

"How do you happen to be here?" she asked.

I outlined my career from itinerant musician to itinerant consultant, explaining that my present occupation was almost exactly like my songwriting career, except that as a consultant, I play a differently shaped guitar. I might not be writing songs now, but I am delivering the same messages I conveyed in my songs.

She was delighted with my story. "So, you've always told stories, then?" she continued.

"Yes," I replied, explaining that I have always been able to use words in unusual ways.

"I noticed that you tell stories more than you tell people what they are supposed to learn," she replied. "I like that."

I explained my strong belief that no one can tell adults anything as powerfully as they can tell it to themselves. "I just give them an opportunity and they do the rest," I explained.

"Well, you're what my mother called a Witness," she observed.

"A Witness?" I questioned. "What's that?"

"My mother taught me that there are many roles that people can play in others' lives," she said. "Some are givers and some are takers, some spread joy and others misery. One of the most powerful roles," she continued, "is the Witness. The Witness observes and shares what he sees. I now realize that you have been doing this all week, just observing and sharing what you see."

I had no clever response. I remember taking in her description deeply, checking its credentials, and savoring this curious possibility. Could I be a Witness? I wondered.

I don't remember the following few minutes. I must have been processing her suggestion so strenuously that I missed whatever was going on in the foreground. Lunch probably arrived, and we might have eaten around this silence. I returned a few minutes later with an appreciation.

"Thank you," I said with a little wavering in my voice, catching her eye as she looked up from her sandwich. "Thank you."

"You're very welcome," she smiled in reply.

We went on to engage in a conversation more typical of my one-on-one meetings. Her work. Her career. Her aspirations. Her interests. I was present and listening, but I was engaging differently than I had before she offered a name for my purpose. I was observing, understanding that I was absorbing important information for sharing later. I was a Witness!

Few could be more poorly suited to this calling. I cannot remember the color of my own shoes without sneaking a quick peek. I never remember faces. I rarely recall names. I didn't know what to call her blouse color when I was looking at it, and I have no memory of it now. I absorb impressions. Fuzzy. Diffuse. Meaning-rich and detail-poor. I could never tell a detective if the perpetrator wore a windbreaker or a pea coat, sneakers or wing tips. He might have sprouted wings and flown away, for all I usually recall. But I can remember the meaning I made of the experience, and I unfailingly remember how that meaning relates to other of my experiences stored before.

I witness meanings, not events. I postulate and project, consider and reframe. I make sense of this world. Then I pass my sense on as stories. I witness.

Being a consultant sometimes means being a Witness. We observe and try to make sense of what we see, passing the meaning we've discovered on to the others who have different roles to play. I travel constantly. I read continually. I meet people from many different places who are fulfilling many different responsibilities. I am a connector between them. I tell stories that bridge the illusory spaces between people, helping them discover again how very similar we all are. I reassure, reminding people what they already know but need some reinforcement to acknowledge. I watch and I tell my stories.

I remain enormously grateful to that woman for offering a name for my purpose. I have considered many times the power she passed along in her brief observation. I have concluded that she must also be fulfilling a purpose. She is a Namer. She has the gift that allows her to name others' purposes. As a Namer, she offers names for consideration. I'm sure not everyone she offers a name to accepts the offer. Not all to whom I witness can hear my stories. The timing must be right. The story must match the situation. All in its own time.

For those who have not yet found their purpose, keep watch. Pay attention. A Namer is offering something you have not heard. Listen. Consider. Then choose and proceed with passion.

DISCOVERING WHAT I WANT

When I discovered what I wanted, it was very close to home. I wanted to witness. I could consult and consult well, and over time I would become a master trainer, too, but never simply for the sake of teaching. Neither my consulting nor my training assignments are ends unto themselves. They are rich mediums within which I can observe. What I can observe, I can write about. Whatever I do, I am doing it to gather material.

Until Larry posed his pesky question and introduced me to my wall, I had convinced myself that doing what I really wanted wouldn't support me. Encountering the wall changed my frame of reference from one that insisted I couldn't make a living doing what I wanted into one that insisted I couldn't make a living *without* doing what I wanted. No wonder I was dizzy! And when I can slow down enough to not hasten quickly by, each new project reintroduces me to the haunting question "What do I want?" My wall reappears for consideration every time. Sometimes I choose differently, because each situation brings a unique set of opportunities and challenges. I don't always pursue a Witness role.

Larry died two years after introducing me to my wall. I visit his grave whenever I'm in Silicon Valley. I feel as if I'm visiting a shrine. I give him a quick status report, introduce him to significant new folks in my life, and leave a symbolic Koosh ball, the toy he always fidgeted with when we had our rambling talks. My first experience with Larry introduced me to my now-obvious wall. I had always convinced myself whenever I had met this wall before that I could not have what I wanted. Larry argued otherwise. My witnessing started with this insight. So did my purposeful professional life. Larry insisted that I had to acknowledge what I wanted before I could engage in meaningful work. He required that I use every engagement as a medium for pursuing my purpose. He introduced me to my wall, but he also gave me the clue I needed to live with it.

I now see Larry's face smirking in the back of the room whenever I introduce my workshop participants to their walls. As I encourage them to help their colleagues "find their project within your project," Larry's impish eyes invade the space. His shadow lurks, Koosh ball in hand, whenever I suggest that the hardest question they'll ever ask their project community members is "What do you want?" No other question has so transformed my life. It will stymie and transform them, and a few of their fellows, too, if they can hasten slowly long enough to face their walls. I cram this simple lesson into a single workshop afternoon, knowing that it might need a lifetime to fully sink in.

I want to be clear when I ask this question, "What do you want?" I do not ask it to create an obligation between us. I could have answered Larry's question, as some of the less successful partners in the firm responded to it, by saying that I wanted a pile of money. I am not now, nor will I ever be, Daddy Warbucks. I do not have, nor do I want to have, a pocketful of payoff cash. I do not want or need another obligation, so please don't misunderstand my intentions when I ask you, "What do you want?" *It's your job, not my job or anyone else's job, to give you what you want.*

Before the beginning of every project, we make bids and take offers, we draft contracts and reach agreements. These are the necessary obligation-making activities that are never really sufficient to fuel any project. Masters promise rewards if their projects meet objectives, and these lures easily obscure a subtler and far more important consideration. In these negotiations, the agreements focus upon one party's satisfying another party. My question asks how you will use this assignment for satisfying yourself.

Projects succeed and projects fail—either way, projects eventually end. Project work brings the certainty that you are working yourself out of a job. This easily translates into working yourself out of a life unless you know how to use the project to make your life. Every assignment offers both obligation and opportunity. We usually focus so intently upon the obligation that we miss the opportunity to use the assignment as a medium for pursuing what we truly want for ourselves.

Every assignment carries within it the possibility for pursuing my purpose, although I always have the power to undermine this possibility. The old adage says, "You can have what you want or all of the reasons why you can't have what you want. Choose one." Every assignment challenges me to acknowledge this unsettling truth and to renew my liberating choice.

I have to be clear about what I want, though, to pursue it. Gaining this clarity has been a lifelong struggle for me. When I was young, I wanted to keep my options open. Later it seemed as though I'd exhausted all of my options. Somewhere in between insisting upon latitude and living a longitudinal life, I lost my belief that I could pursue what I wanted, settling instead for what I had.

Most of my Masters have been good at helping me lose my focus. They offered compelling compromises. These payoffs easily nudged aside my pursuit of my real purpose. They almost as easily nudged aside the belief that I should even have a purpose. When I engaged at the obligation level, depleting myself for their payoffs, I rewarded myself only with ever-deepening meaninglessness.

I learned as a small child something you might have learned, too. I learned that I am supposed to sacrifice myself for my work. Asking myself what I want feels wrongheaded. I'm supposed to ask what my Master wants me to do, not what I want from my experience. Isn't work supposed to be about doing someone else's bidding, not about pursuing my own? Yet, without an answer to this question, my contribution lacks an essential juiciness. And without this focus, both my client and I get less from the experience. If answering this question will give more to both of us, it isn't just self-serving—it serves us both well.

I made up stories about the gallantry of self-sacrifice, but those projects felt like death marches anyway. What can ensure against a death march? I'm convinced that obligation can't. Real death-march insurance requires that I create my own payoff, using my project assignment as a medium to pursue what I want. No Master can supply purpose. I have to discover for myself what I want if I expect to pursue a meaningful purpose.

JUICINESS

OK, I admit it. What I'm really doing when I ask this question is hatching a conspiracy. No, I'm not plotting anything illegal. I don't intend to overthrow anything. I am merely offering the possibility to conspire—as Webster defines it, "to act in harmony toward a common end." I will not insist. I don't want to steal anyone's choices. I intend only to remind you of the opportunity for you to use this assignment as a medium for chasing purpose.

This properly focuses attention. We might otherwise simply start hastening toward the Master's goal and miss the opportunity to pursue something personally meaningful.

YOUR OXYGEN MASK FIRST!

I had ridden on hundreds of commercial airline flights before realizing what the flight attendants were really saying before take-off. They said, "Put on your own oxygen mask before helping others." Help myself first? This seems self-serving, like asking myself what I want, but how can I expect to help anyone else breathe if I'm suffocating?

No methodology suggests starting projects by answering the question "What do I want?" Perhaps they should. But I swear that like the announcements flight attendants make to cabins full of hastening and uninterested travelers, the message would not often get through. This inquiry must eventually become a question for you to ask and answer for yourself.

I ask each person on my projects what he or she wants. This often yields the same reaction I gave Larry over breakfast. I've pointed out their wall, and it casts a huge and encumbering shadow for a while. Clients have accused me of being overbearing for suggesting that they could use their assignment as a means of pursuing what they want. "What part of considering what you want seems oppressive to you?" I ask, even though I well understand the feelings churning inside them. I'm merely trying to hatch a meaningful conspiracy, the medium within which we can really "act in harmony toward a common end."

I ask this question to encourage juiciness, to chase away the flat, dry, cynical efforts too often found on projects. It's too hip to be cynical. Cynics are wounded optimists. They are ex-gamboling lambs who have had too many wolf encounters. Cynics have chosen to embrace all the reasons why they cannot pursue what they want. A clear idea of my purpose makes excellent wolf insurance. I can make my part in this messy world better by using the world, whatever the mess, as a medium for pursuing what I want. Setbacks and disappointments are simply plot twists on the way from here to there. Cynics outsmart themselves, sidestepping their own most meaningful potential.

The cynic might just be a poor punctuator. A colleague told me a story about a friend who stormed into her office one day. She complained that she had finally figured out that her mother had been right after all, damn it! She said she had always, until that day, disagreed with her mother's claim that everything always turned out for the best. That day, though, she'd discovered that her mother's belief depended upon where she acknowledged the endings of her experiences.

"If I call a bad time an ending, then things don't always turn out for the best," her mother explained. "But if I look at a bad time and call it a middle rather than an end, things don't ever have to turn out badly. I just have to wait until the next natural uptick in the experience, call that an ending, punctuate there, and I'm in complete control of my experiences' always turning out well."

I want each of my projects to be play, the front behind which I have juicy experiences. All projects evaporate when their product "ships." In this way, project work becomes beautifully analogous to life. On the face of it, you struggle and then it ends. Project work spawns cynics because it often turns out differently than expected, disappointing original ideals. Furthermore, people doing organizational work build and maintain permanent fiefdoms, while those participating in project work create things that will pass into someone else's hands, never to return.

I can no longer fool myself into believing that any Master should be responsible for providing my purpose. I've felt robbed every time I've delegated this responsibility to an employer. I have to acknowledge that I was always the thief, though. I can and do work with others. Others pay me for this work. What's the difference now? I'm always pursuing something for myself in the trade. I give better than fair effort for my pay, and I'm always using the assignment as a medium for pursuing something juicy for myself. I use my project to pursue, rather than barter away, my purpose. The resulting juiciness shows.

"GOD BLESS ME! BUT THE ELEPHANT IS VERY LIKE A WALL!"

What do I want? The question, when presented, seems very much like a wall. Even now, I have no automatic response. The question persists and inconveniences me. My answer lies in simply acknowledging my intentions. This first feels like a huge limitation. But paring away all the reasons why I can't pursue what I want usually reveals my purpose, an intention that transforms my wall into a meaningful foundation.

I can reasonably predict a series of walls, each a dedication test, stretching between me and my project's objective. My encounters with these walls can deplete or renew me. When I'm powered by pursuing a juicy purpose, I am not so depleted by my efforts. When I forget to also dedicate the effort to my own best interest, the work just exhausts me.

I am that one at the start of your project who cannot quite get moving yet. I need a milling-around period. Give me some time to consider what I'm doing here. If you insist that I hasten quickly on your way, I will come. I will come and I will help you forget why you're doing this work, too. I prefer to have a purpose, and I need some time to consider this engagement before I can engage. I don't really need your enticements. If I cannot find my purpose within this project, I am likely to decline the opportunity. Even if you offer me rewards, I am better off walking away if I cannot find anything juicy here. I appreciate your patience with me.

What is your purpose? What do you want?

THE SPEAR

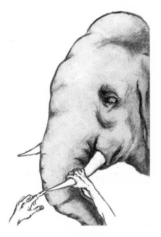

4

The Second, feeling of the tusk,

Cried, "Ho! what have we here,

So very round and smooth and sharp?

To me 'tis mighty clear

This wonder of an Elephant

Is very like a spear!"

—From "The Blind Men and the
Elephant," by John Godfrey Saxe

THE TALE OF A VERY BAD SOLDIER

I don't know much about being a soldier. I worked very hard at avoiding military service. I conscientiously objected to the notion that the military could settle anything, or could make anyone safer, especially with me as a part of it. Above all, I objected to the idea of blindly following anyone else's orders, no matter how much sense the orders seemed to make to him. My head still echoes with stories of the Somme, Antietam, and Gallipoli, where generals' delusions played out into fields of freshly planted conscripts. I would have made a very bad soldier, and I clearly had no business in the military. I was surprised when my draft board agreed with my self-assessment and decided that it didn't want me!

I learned a little bit about projects in that process.

I came of age in the late '60s, when almost everyone I knew had grown to oppose the Vietnam War effort. I was dedicated to staying out of the service, so I worked hard to keep my options open. When I registered for the draft, I requested every available hearing, procedure, and due process. The draft board's Evil Secretary (or so I called her) scowled at me as she reviewed my completed forms. A few weeks later, I was ordered to appear for a qualifying physical examination in a city 200 miles away. I prepared for the examination by fasting for several days, arriving, after a long bus ride and a sleepless night, just as fit as most other eighteen-year-olds. The doctors, none of whom spoke enough English to understand anything any of us "inductees" said, evaluated us as if we were horseflesh. I was classified 1-A, qualified for immediate induction.

This evaluation process reminds me of the "resource allocation" processes employed to populate projects, where leaders assess potential contributors according to superficial characteristics without ever understanding what strengths or weaknesses each might want to bring to the assignment. No one thinks to ask what the inductee wants out of his or her work. The inductees might neglect even to ask themselves. The subject just doesn't come up. I cannot today engage in these exercises without remembering how demeaning it felt to be one of those horses at auction.

A few months later, thanks to a remarkably low lottery number, the mail brought a notice for me to appear for induction into the service. I read it and simply threw it away. The phone rang on the day I had been ordered to appear. The Evil Secretary at the draft board was calling to find out where I was. "I am home," I brazenly told her, "and I will not be down today." Hadn't I requested the option of exercising my rights to a full hearing with the draft board before being inducted? Her end of the line grew silent. After a moment, she came back on the line. "Well ... yes ... Sir (she called me "Sir"!), I ... do ... see ... that you requested ... a hearing. We will get ... back to you with a date."

Whew! This experience reinforced my idea of keeping my options open. Especially when doubting another's judgment, I choose variety. I had at the time no idea what any of the options on those forms meant, but I suspected that the more options I chose, the more choices I would retain. This may seem unpatriotic to those who simply answered the call. This might make me a very bad soldier, but when a plan doesn't make sense to me, I'm pretty much paralyzed in the face of it. I am as a result very sensitive to the need to make meaningful plans—not ones that simply make sense to me, but ones that make sense to those who will have to follow them. The system that selected, processed, and ordered me around felt designed simply to dehumanize me, and it rendered me nearly incapable of complying. I didn't like being treated as an object. I work very hard today to avoid objectifying my project team members.

I didn't know then that I was acting in what modern systems scientists would characterize as a highly ethical manner. Cyberneticist Heinz von Foerster characterized a healthy human system as one that reveres variety over similarity, choice over command. He proposed an ethical imperative, "Act always so as to increase the number of choices." My introduction to "bad" soldier behavior, wrestling with the draft, would serve me very well as I began assuming fuzzy responsibilities on complex projects.

The Evil Secretary called back a few days later. I could argue my case before the draft board in six weeks. After considering the options, I decided to pursue a "nonmilitary conscientious objector" classification. The draft-resister literature rated nonmilitary CO as next-to-impossible to secure, but this classification best described my situation. I found myself in the curious position of arguing in favor of becoming employed for two years, at something like half minimum wage, as a civilian orderly in a military hospital. This outcome seemed superior to the option of becoming a good soldier, abrogating my own judgment. I felt that I could retain my sanity changing bedpans. Following orders looked like another matter.

Sometimes, standing up for myself leaves me pretty far hunched over. Yet I shudder to think how much farther bent over discounting my own judgment might have left me. Obtaining the nonmilitary CO classification would leave me in what might seem to anyone else a completely compromised position. I pursued it anyway. Not because I was out to destroy myself, but because I wanted to retain some choices for myself, as any truly bad soldier might.

Then the most remarkable things started happening. Unexpected allies emerged as word got out around my hometown. A friend's father, a United States district judge, volunteered to write a letter supporting my petition. A teacher, an Annapolis graduate and decorated World War II hero, also volunteered. My father, a marine for a time before being mustered out on a medical discharge, came in strongly supportive, volunteering to testify before the board. And so it went. A community went public on my behalf.

This response echoes my experience since. Leaving my options open created possibilities for unanticipated allies to appear. I could not have imagined such support behind me until I looked over my shoulder and found it there. I've since grown to rely upon these surprising legions. Given half an opportunity, people step in to help. Showing an ounce of courage, asserting a pinch of humanity, exposing just a bit of my true self brings the partisans out from hiding. Leave the door open a crack and support slips in.

I reported as ordered to the next meeting of the draft board. The board, a half-dozen old men sitting around a circular conference table, reviewed my paperwork. The Evil Secretary hovered nearby. Individual board members questioned me.

What if I were given the option of either entering the military or going to prison? Which would I choose?

"That would be *you* choosing, not me," I replied. "I've already told you that I object to entering the military. I guess if you think that putting me in prison will make the world a better place, that's your decision. But I won't be party to it."

What if terrorists kidnapped my grandmother and threatened to kill her? Wouldn't I want to kill them first? they continued.

"Not particularly. I don't see what either killing would accomplish. I guess I'd wish Grandma well and hope for the best," I replied.

The questions ranged over my morality and the guilt they expected me to feel for letting others do "my" work. To tell the truth, I felt morally superior to that group of old men plotting to ship young men off to war. My morality was never the point, and I didn't feel guilty for myself but sad for all of the compliant ones, the ones who hadn't chosen the opportunity to assert their personal preferences. This was tough work because the board members and

I had such different values. It was as if, when we looked at the elephant before us, they saw a spear where I saw a walking stick. We engaged in a dialogue of the deaf, each asserting his perspective to the unhearing ears of the other.

The board interviewed my father separately. I do not know what he told them. The hearing ended with the promise that I would be notified of their decision by mail. Tick ... tick ... tick ... I felt as if I had strapped myself to a time bomb.

There were times during this hearing when I simply wanted to concede. This rigmarole was completely inconveniencing, embarrassing, even humiliating. I felt as though I must be questioning God, and the board members treated me as if I were a deliberately subversive heretic. I was terrified of the consequences of my innocent assertion, even though asserting was completely within my rights. I felt paranoid, as if I should be slinking out of the board meeting, hoping no one would see my exit.

I have never had a project assignment where I did not have to assert myself through a similar fog of embarrassment and self-doubt. I have sometimes caved under this pressure and chosen to just "go along to get along." Curious results. Whenever I chose to go along and be an unquestioningly compliant soldier, my project ended up being the worse for it. Going along bartered away useful alternatives, as well as my mobility, for no more than the temporary appearance of tranquillity. The resulting poorly secured lid usually blew off later, anyway. Under von Foerster's Ethical Imperative, going along to get along amounts to unethical behavior, but bucking the flow doesn't necessarily feel very powerful or reassuring in the moment.

Two weeks after the meeting, I received notice of the board members' approval of my nonmilitary CO classification. They had believed me! I could fulfill my obligation by serving two years as a civilian employee of a military hospital. There was only one catch. I had to find a hospital willing to accept me. I hadn't understood this wrinkle. This stipulation made being a conscientious objector like being on unemployment. I had to report monthly to the Evil Secretary and demonstrate that I had diligently sought opportunities to fulfill my obligation. I had never been on unemployment, so this was a new and completely surprising experience. My life went on hold as I set about securing my own employment as a conscientious objector.

Projects never end as planned. Just as in my later project work, I got what I wanted from the draft board, only to learn that what I got was very different from what I'd expected. I retained choice and received an unexpected responsibility along with it. Choice always brings responsibility. Leaving options open often results in unanticipated outcomes. I was supposed to be both the prospective employee and my own employment agency. I had never been in the employment agency business before. I was going to have to invent a way to satisfy this obligation.

I tried applying at the local Veterans Administration hospital, only to be told that I could not work there because it was less than sixty miles from my permanent home address. (Fine print stipulated that the work be done at least sixty miles away from my permanent home address.) My life became a continuous job search as I scoured the local library, gathering addresses of Veterans Administration hospitals. I painstakingly wrote, in my best but nearly illegible handwriting, each introductory letter:

Dear Major McGillicutty: [This person usually had a rank designation, which didn't mean anything to me, preceding his name. They were all members of the military.]

My draft board has recently designated me 1-H, a nonmilitary conscientious objector. This 1-H classification requires me to seek civilian employment at a military hospital located at least sixty miles from my permanent home address. Please forward by return mail any employment opportunities you might have available for someone of my classification.

Sincerely,

David Schmaltz

I equally painstakingly (and illegibly) wrote a duplicate of each original letter for the Evil Secretary's files. At the end of each month, I reported to the draft board to show to the Evil Secretary the list of hospitals I had contacted and the copies of the letters I had sent. She certified that I had met my quota for the month and sent me on my way. (Failure to meet the contact quota would have changed my classification to 1-A, leaving me subject to immediate induction.)

Bad soldiers have to tolerate mindless bureaucracy, just the same as good soldiers. Both serve on missions that sometimes shift into the opposite of the original intention. My service to my country consisted of writing letters to faceless administrators, offering what each could easily refuse. The system didn't intend this outcome, I didn't intend this outcome, but nonetheless the system reinforced this result once it had induced it. I adapted, as both good and bad soldiers must. I was surprised. I had expected to be simply snatched up and assigned to some dismal backwater. Looking back, I realize that I *had been* assigned to a dismal backwater. I found myself trapped in an absurd and inescapable limbo. Thinking that any month might be my last month in freedom, I couldn't take permanent work. I worked casual-labor jobs and one-night stands.

No one responded to any of my letters. I don't know why. The country was suffering through high unemployment at that time, and I imagined laid-off professionals filling all the available hospital-orderly positions. Most likely, my requests were discarded upon receipt. Eventually, the Evil Secretary allowed me to submit by mail my monthly list of contacted hospitals and the copies of my letters. Later, the whole thing seemed to go into suspension, as we agreed that I was paradoxically both conforming with the requirements and unable to fulfill them.

The Selective Service law had no requirement for military hospital administrators to hire conscientious objectors. I had no way of knowing this when I petitioned the draft board for reclassification. I was just being myself. I'm confident that no one on the draft board knew about the hospital administrators' practice, either. If anyone there had known, the board most certainly would not have designated anyone 1-H, because that designation would in practice oblige every conscientious objector to engage in a seemingly endless, meaningless dance. Come to think of it, my experience as a bad soldier was remarkably similar to the experiences of many good soldiers. The difference? I never accepted that anyone else knew better for me. This attitude helped me cope when it turned out, as it so often has in my life, that no one knew better than I did about myself. This difference has been a defining one for me and for my projects.

I was standing in the kitchen of an apartment in Seattle's University District on the morning when the president announced the suspension of the military draft. In that moment, my obligation evaporated. This wasn't the end of my paradoxical experiences at the hands of bureaucracy, but it was the end of this chapter of them. Because I had been unsuccessful in my many, many attempts to satisfy the letter of the law, I was finally no longer obliged to satisfy it. I've often noticed since that insisting upon *exactly* satisfying my vision guarantees that I don't get what I want. Organizations insisting upon specific implementation alternatives create such inescapable contradictions for both their good and bad soldiers. If that system could have relaxed any one of its many rules, its intent could have been satisfied. The sixty-mile rule, for instance, guaranteed that strangers would have to make the system work, and they could not. I found ways to cope, to preserve my own sanity, but no effort on my part could transform the system's constraints into anything but endless paradox.

This experience conditioned me to continue being a very bad soldier. When my five-times great-grandfather mustered his Virginia militia company during the Revolutionary War, something like a quarter of those called did not appear. Some were fined for their trouble. Others were acknowledged as Quakers and either assigned to a Quaker company or excused from service altogether. Quakers, you see, wouldn't follow orders. They didn't believe in following another man's directions.

Others easily follow commands. They expect concrete direction. They feel something missing when they do not receive it. They accept the world as a system of hierarchies, with leaders and followers naturally blending into ranks and files. I have never experienced the world this way.

I must, though, if I am to get along in this world, acknowledge that others, perhaps most, will see something different from what I see when we look at the same elephant. Deafness greets our explanations until we discover that correctness of perspective isn't even beside the point. My assertions make no more sense to you than yours do to me. Expecting you to behave according to my definition of good-soldier "reasonable" can't help but confuse and disappoint both of us.

MONITORING MY METAPHORS

Attending a weekend retreat with a group of old friends, I felt very warmly received, reveling in the natural affinity between us. After one particularly touching conversation, I commented that this group felt just like family to me. I didn't notice anything un-usual at the time, but my comment prompted one in the group to emotionally check out. I later learned in the middle of a minor disagreement that my colleague had taken offense at my suggestion. He trembled as he told me that in his family, his father beat him and his mother every night. As a child he lived in constant fear of the certainty of these beatings, and this was what family meant to him. "This *is not* like a family for me, and I don't want it to be like a family," he said with understandable passion.

Even an analogy as seemingly harmless as family can wreak havoc for some around you. I have long experience innocently backing my metaphorical truck over others, telling my story in ways that seemed to wound or offend or alienate. I rarely intended these outcomes. How could I possibly have known that anyone would take offense?

In one workshop, I innocently characterized passion as being like Al Jolson down on one knee singing "Mammy." Someone reported to the human resources vice president, "David is using racial slurs," without first mentioning anything to me. I was asked to report to the VP's office, where I was dressed down for destroy-ing the effectiveness of the training by using racist metaphors. I wasn't using racist metaphors, just metaphors. I told him that the racism must have been in the head of the meaning maker and that no offense was intended or even imagined! I suggested that he speak with the person who was polluting her own experience with such scathing interpretations. Still, I have permanently deleted that metaphor from my repertoire.

We are all learning to be more sensitive in selecting metaphors in the workplace. Who hasn't cringed when watching a character in an old movie use a term that today clearly demonstrates race, gender, or class bias? Remembering some of the terms my grandparents used in everyday conversation can make me blush. When I graduated from high school, women were commonly referred to as "girls," a term I wouldn't be caught dead using today. Our characterizations are the honest products of our learning, the result of exposure, repetition, and innocent comparison. When I first began leading others, my company sent me to a sensitivity class intended to make me more aware of the ways in which others might interpret my language. I was shocked at how much trouble my word choices could create for myself and my company. I learned to carefully monitor my metaphors.

"TO ME 'TIS MIGHTY CLEAR, THIS WONDER OF AN ELEPHANT IS VERY LIKE A SPEAR!"

The metaphors we casually employ can undermine our projects. As the story of my experiences with the military might suggest, I am particularly sensitive to one class of metaphors that are commonly used to describe projects. Predictable things happen when we start describing our projects as battles. People behave as if they are soldiers. Directions become orders. Work becomes fierce competition. Plans become immutable. Enemies emerge. We and our opponents become less than human, shrinking as individuals. Our Technicolor world fades into opaque wrongs and colorless rights, when our success requires a palette filled with possibility.

War metaphors limit a project's potential. We are unlikely from within these blinding descriptions to find opportunities for building communities that include both "us" and "them," choosing instead to build defensive perimeters that entrap us more than they protect us. War metaphors encourage fierce competition, just as if our engagements were a matter of life and death, when they rarely are. Staying true to centuries of military tradition, we pursue innovation but miss opportunities to transform while we follow apparently mindless orders, hurrying up to wait.

Our projects are not wars. They do not require the good-soldier obedience that a battlefield might oblige us to provide. Our leaders are not our generals; they are not the clever strategists we might aspire them to be. If you were raised on a diet of command and control, this notion must seem ludicrous. After all, what could be more reasonable than for a commander to order his soldiers to "take that hill"?

When I hear this order, I ask myself, and perhaps the fellow in the foxhole—er, cubicle—next to me, "Why?" I don't really care in that moment if I'm being insubordinate. I need to know the intent behind the order. The order gives me a weak target, and it doesn't help me grasp the intention behind the objective. What will we have after we've taken the hill that we don't have now? What's our next move? Where does this movement fit into a broader strategy?

In classic command-control theory, we are encouraged to "stuff" these questions. "Ours is not to reason why, ours is but to do or die" was as wrongheaded a notion in the notoriously disastrous Charge of the Light Brigade as it is today. Ours must be most definitely to reason why, since the alternative just might be to do *and* die. In the flat-earth world imagined by the Father of Scientific Management and reverberating in today's project management practices is the view that management's right and proper role is to pare down available options to the single best one and enforce good-soldier compliance around that option. Our Earth isn't flat as our ancestors' theories assumed, so narrowing options quite unavoidably undermines our project's potential. Where the Earth is filled with variety, as it surely is, potential becomes the true source of our unfolding success. Narrowing potential becomes simply destructive. And von Foerster would have to consider such narrowing unethical, too.

Can we ask our questions: Why? What will we have? What next? How should a good soldier interpret the order to "take that hill"? One might set out dangerously exposed up the face of the hill while another sneaks safely around the back. One might try to isolate the hill, while another calls in artillery. Still another requests a helicopter assault team's support. Without further clarification, without an understanding of the intention behind and the meaning in front of the directive, obedient soldiers are left to do bad soldiering. The bad soldier, the one who questions the meaning and intention behind the order, is the one most likely to satisfy it. Interesting contradiction.

Yet this blind man, like many working on projects today, "sees" a spear when he just as easily might "see" a walking stick, a tent pole, or a fishing rod. Spears are thrusting and throwing weapons used to maintain distance. With them we can threaten, build defensive perimeters, and fend off others. Heavy, awkward, and inconvenient to carry, spears, like most defensive weapons, prevent us from carrying much of anything else. Unless we need to defend ourselves, we would be foolish to disadvantage ourselves by bringing along a spear.

Consider imagining your perspective as something other than a defensive weapon. Transform your spear into a walking stick, a tent pole, or a fishing rod. As a walking stick, the spear could ease your trek. As a tent pole, it could help shelter you. As a fishing rod, it could help feed and sustain you. Most projects need an easier trek more than they need a defensive perimeter, a better night's rest more than they need a throwing weapon, and sustenance more than they need to maintain the distance between themselves and anyone else.

When you hear another casually deploying these self-destructive metaphors, consider commenting, "Is this *really* a war?" "Are our customers *really* the enemy?" Often, simply commenting on the incongruity breaks the trance. Behaving as if your implement were not the spear others imagine it to be, using it in distinctly unspearlike ways, can also open possibilities for untangling others' tenacious spells. Such commenting and modeling is ethical behavior, intended to increase the number of available choices.

Our projects today need contributors who will not simply bring a compliant, good-soldier mind-set to their assignments. We need "bad" soldiers, those who will

- Insist upon choices
- Leave their options open
- Question authority
- Tolerate well the potential embarrassment and inconvenience that come with using their own judgment to temper the orders they receive

We need "bad" leaders, too. Leaders who

- Leave an array of implementation alternatives open to their teams
- Accept results other than *exactly* what they first expected

As I learned when wrestling with the draft board's unyielding requirements, holding rigidly to a single implementation alternative effectively prevents anything from being accomplished.

The ethics of our complicated project work require that we act always so as to increase the number of choices available to us, choices in both approach and result. This doesn't mean that we should not decide upon definite courses of action. It does, however, mean we understand that each course of action is a choice from among an unimaginably vast number of choices, that each grand plan is one of many possible paths from here to there, and that another plan can always be created should this one prove unworkable. We cannot insist upon bad soldiering, because blindly obeying an order to be a bad soldier can only create good soldiers (a paradox). If others are to be effective as bad soldiers, they must take up their own campaigns, their own ethical initiative, however seemingly foolhardy, as some might consider my campaign against the draft board to have been foolhardy. *We must be prepared to be fools for our own good judgment or suffer under the judgment of fools.*

Some will insist upon being compliant soldiers, expecting their leaders to direct them along straight and narrow paths. These are unethical expectations because they limit the available options; they exclude the essential variety that each brings to his or her project assignment. We need more than horseflesh on our projects today— we need the active, questioning judgment of every participating individual.

Perhaps your elephant isn't as much like a spear as it first appeared. Your projects are not wars. Your project work requires healthy injections of your own judgment because blind compliance undermines success. How will you choose to fulfill your ethical responsibility to bring your best bad-soldier judgment into play?

THE SNAKE

5

The Third approached the animal,
And happening to take
The squirming trunk within his hands,
Thus boldly up he spake:
"I see," quoth he, "the Elephant
Is very like a snake!"

—From "The Blind Men and the
Elephant," by John Godfrey Saxe

WHO'S HERE WITH YOU?

There's an old folktale about a man who met a snake while walking down a road.

"Excuse me," said the man, "but you look exactly like a snake."

"That's because I am a snake," replied the snake. "But I am not like other snakes. I am not poisonous, or constrictive, or the sort of individual who would harm anyone."

"Oh, how interesting," continued the man. "I've never met a kind snake before. Would you like to come home with me to dinner?"

"I'd be charmed," said the snake.

So the man picked up the snake and took him home to have dinner with his family. The man tried to calm his family's concerns when they saw him bringing a snake into the house. "This is a different sort of snake," he explained. "Not the poisonous or constrictive or in any way harmful kind. There's no need to be alarmed."

In spite of his reassurances, his family refused to sit at the same table with the snake. The man, bull-headed, sat down at the table with the snake, anyway. It was no surprise to anyone in the family when halfway through the entrée a minor tussle occurred, and the snake bit the man.

"How could you?" the man pleaded, as his wife called for an ambulance.

"You knew I was a snake when you picked me up," replied the snake as he slithered away.

TRUSTING SNAKES

When I was a kid, there was a book on the shelf at home titled *You Can Trust a Communist to Be a Communist*. I was always fascinated by the title because it seemed to contradict itself. I learned in school that Communists were untrustworthy, so I understood the title to mean that I could trust someone to be untrustworthy. This was a much more powerful and provocative statement than *Communists Are Untrustworthy* or *Don't Trust Communists*.

I could make the same statement about snakes. You can trust a snake to be a snake. The man in the opening story took the word of someone whose word had always been unreliable. He knew it was a snake when he picked it up. He should have known better than to trust it. Only fools expect snakes to be trustworthy. He was a fool.

What causes a snake not to be a snake? Perhaps more important, how can you tell if you're holding on to a snake? I have been bitten a few times—sometimes by known snakes and sometimes by "snakes in the grass"—snakes that I didn't recognize as such until after I had been bitten. Snakes are snakes, but not all snakes look like snakes at first. Some look like anything but a snake until later.

A good general rule might be never to trust snakes to be trustworthy. There can be no assumption of a covenant between a person and a snake. If it's not in the contract, the snake will never feel obliged to comply. So if snakes are untrustworthy and one cannot always tell if he is dealing with a snake until after he's been bitten, I might logically conclude that I should treat everyone as if she is a snake until proven otherwise.

Some people live like this, drafting the prenuptial agreement before beginning the relationship. Security personnel observe everything. Nondisclosure agreements are signed before business cards are exchanged. Maximum-security precautions are observed at all times. Briefcases are searched on entry and exit.

I recently completed a workshop at a very successful technology company where security was extreme. Sign in, bags searched, escorted while inside, sign out. I could not leave the training room, even to go to the men's room two doors down, without an escort. My partner was trapped in the lobby during one lunch break and had to call me at my cell phone in the training room to ask me to send an escort down for her. What was going on here? It seemed like paranoia to me. Someone must have been badly bitten in the past. I found this ever-present security unsettling. I felt insecure, as if I were in the company of snakes, or worse yet, as if I might be suspected of being a snake when I never was—and never would have been. When we assume that we're dealing with snakes, everyone becomes a suspect. Everyone, in effect, becomes a snake. We insist upon it.

We can become too security-conscious. There were so many checkpoints and checklists at that company that some of the most important elements of security were overlooked. No one asked us to sign a nondisclosure agreement, for instance, even though we spent several days dissecting the most intimate details of their important projects. In the swarm of secure-making, no one asked me not to disclose the secrets I learned.

I have no idea what of all I heard was supposed to be secret, anyway. In one workshop, I mentioned a project name that had come up in a past workshop and during the next break was soundly chastised by someone from the same company, who claimed that I had disclosed a proprietary secret by mentioning that project's name,

Mr. Potato Head! I didn't mention the project's objective, novel technology, cost, resource allocation, or difficulties—just the name, Mr. Potato Head. I felt terrible, as if I had disclosed some huge secret. But to tell the truth, it felt more as if the chastiser was blowing an insignificant something out of proportion. I was no snake. No one had been bitten. Perhaps he had bitten himself? I wondered.

SORRY SORT OF SAFETY

Everyone looks like a snake to the dedicated snake hunter. Perhaps we become what we chase, easily assuming that everyone else must be what we are pursuing, too. I characterize this attitude not as better safe than sorry but the sorriest sort of safety.

For those who expect to see only snakes, the world has to be a dangerous place. Security forces might inconvenience, but they are absolutely necessary. "Only the paranoid survive" becomes a self-sealing belief for the truly paranoid. If you are paranoid and you have survived so far, why question the belief? The sorriest sort of safety seems necessary, prudent, and even wise.

WHO BUYS DISK DRIVES?

My mentor and friend J.R Clark once told me that jerks don't buy disk drives. I was skeptical. The disk drive business has always been one of the more cutthroat, skinny-margined businesses in this world. I understood that it attracted jerks who were more interested in trimming their margin than in creating an equitable deal. But J.R persisted in the notion that jerks never buy drives. He explained that when he first started selling peripherals, he noticed that jerks didn't buy drives even if he offered the best performance, price, and delivery schedule. They wouldn't buy for anything! One day, while preparing to visit one of his "jerk" customers, J.R decided to try an experiment. He would find something, anything, to love about the next jerk he visited. Maybe he would admire the way the jerk knotted his tie or the way he organized his desktop; J.R would find something to adore. After an hour of adoration, the "jerk" bought drives! J.R validated this experiment again and again on his way to becoming a top salesman in the disk drive business. When asked how he achieved his success, he'd reply, with a gleam in his eye, "Jerks don't buy drives."

J.R noticed that when he treated his customers as if they were snakes, they easily obliged him by becoming snakes. It took an accident, really, for him to discover that he was the snake maker and not merely the victim in these relationships. It took considerable reinforcement before his mind-set shift became automatic. He had a lot of experience with snakes.

My wife grew up in South Dakota, where snakes are neither poisonous nor constrictive, and she has no "natural" fear of them. She found them to be useful tools for tormenting her sisters when they were small, as she could tolerate picking them up and carrying them around. I was raised where only some of the snakes are poisonous. Most are harmless, yet I have a strong, automatic reaction to finding a snake. I jump and flee.

SNAKE HUNTING

I received an e-mail message from a colleague who complained about the *Peanuts* cartoon character Lucy. He had always disliked the continuing story line in which Lucy held the football for Charlie Brown, exhorting him to run up and kick it. Every time, she pulled the football away at the last moment, leaving Charlie Brown kicking air before landing painfully on his back, seeing stars.

"This cartoon taught me to distrust women," my colleague reported. I was confused. I had never seen a snake in this tableau. I see a large difference between a drawing of a little girl in a comic strip and the class of all female humans, women. Not my colleague. He saw in Lucy's deceit an archetypal representation of some fundamental truth about the relationship between men and women, and he didn't like it. He complained, "I like my role models to be uplifting!"

"Then make more generous interpretations of their actions," I counseled.

I always saw a different archetype in Charlie Brown's relationship with Lucy. Lucy might be a snake, but the significance of this story line for me was never Lucy's deception but Charlie Brown's trust. Even though Lucy has never even once acted in a trustworthy manner, Charlie Brown struggles with his decision to kick the football. His uncertainty represents for me a seed of faith that the future could be different from the past. He struggles and then always decides to give Lucy the benefit of his own doubt. He charges the football, which Lucy then pulls away, laughing maniacally.

Who loses in this scenario? According to my colleague, Charlie Brown loses. "If someone treated my trust like that," he reported, "I'd want to kill them!" He has very strong emotions for an interaction with a Sunday morning comic strip. I always saw Lucy as losing. Lucy represents one of those snakes who, in order to feel equal to others, has to put others one-down from her, as if they were a step behind her on some grand staircase. Lucy puts herself on a pedestal by digging a trench for everyone else. She works too hard! And what does she get out of her effort? Only a moment's satisfaction as her rube stumbles into her carefully crafted pit.

Here's the real question: What does Charlie Brown lose by stumbling into Lucy's pit? I always considered Charlie Brown the winner in these encounters. He clearly struggles each time with his decision to trust again. He struggles and wins, deciding to extend his trust. Then he gets those few moments in which his renewed faith in the outcome propels him forward. Pulling the ball away always seems like a loss for Lucy. She might be elevated by Charlie Brown's tumble, but she doesn't end up any better off than when she started. And Charlie Brown seems overall better off, having had a few moments of exhilaration before a very small tumble. Charlie could have chosen to be safe rather than sorry. He might even have chosen the sorriest sort of safety, one without any exhilaration. He chose the invigorating risk instead.

Charlie Brown loses little. He will trade having the wind knocked out of him for coming to on his back in the middle of a field. His faithful dog will escort him home. Lucy leaves alone with the private knowledge that she outsmarted someone whom she never considered very smart, anyway.

Charlie and Lucy are playing different games. Lucy plays a finite game, where success settles for momentary superiority. She plans a move, executes it, and then concludes that she has won "the game." Lucy feels smart. Charlie Brown's game is not so finite. Trusting today does not decide anything for him about trusting tomorrow, or the next day, or the day after that. Lucy might be a snake, but Charlie Brown was never looking for snakes; he's been looking for excuses to trust. Why? Because such trust becomes its own reward. Charlie Brown's wisdom leaves him looking dumb to those playing a narrower game on a tight little playing field. Charlie becomes the endless fool for Lucy, the mindlessly competitive player, whose time scale never stretches to see the wisdom in looking for excuses to trust those who have proved themselves to be snakes in the past.

Lucy's deceit and defection can't affect Charlie Brown's overall quality of experience. He can at any time choose to experience trust as long as he can assume the risk associated with that choice. When he can accept the risk, he receives in return an immediate boost, as the world seems to become more trustworthy in that moment. What a foolish but useful game.

TIT FOR TAT

In the '80s, Robert Axelrod designed a computer tournament to test the limits of the utility of trust. To do this, he invited authors to submit computer programs designed to compete within what he called an "iterated prisoner's dilemma scenario." The competition paired each program with every other program for twenty iterations of a game called the Prisoner's Dilemma. The Prisoner's Dilemma, an old conundrum, was originally formulated, says Douglas R. Hofstadter in his book *Metamagical Themas*, by Melvin Dresher and Merrill Flood, of the RAND Corporation. A single iteration of the Prisoner's Dilemma plays out the choices of two alleged accomplices who, having been arrested, appear before the district attorney. The DA offers the following deal: If neither cooperates, they will be prosecuted based upon circumstantial evidence, and each will most certainly receive a two-year sentence. Should one implicate the other, however, the implicator will go free and the other will get twenty years. What if both implicate? Four years apiece. Guards then escort the prisoners to consider their choices in separate cells.

Theorists long ago concluded that in a single iteration of this dilemma, implication becomes the best choice. Actually, they used the words "least worst" choice, because there can be no absolute "best" choice—that's why it's called the Prisoner's *Dilemma*, instead of the Prisoner's Problem. Implication becomes the least worst choice because whatever the accomplice chooses, the implicator avoids the worst case, twenty years in jail. But what, asked Robert Axelrod, would emerge as the "least worst" strategy if the situation were repeated twenty times—and with each iteration, both parties remembered what happened the previous time? Charlie Brown, Lucy, and a football come into focus.

Several dozen computer programs were entered into this tournament. Least jail time demonstrated success. Each program interacted with every other program as if it were its accomplice through twenty iterations of the dilemma. Interesting thing, the simplest program won. Another interesting thing, the tournament-winning program didn't win a single individual competition. What was the winning strategy? The successful program, submitted by game master Anatol Rapaport, was called Tit for Tat. Tit for Tat began, Charlie Brown-like, by assuming the best of the accomplice. If, however, the accomplice implicated on the first move, Tit for Tat reciprocated, simply repeating its counterpart's move on the second move and every move thereafter. If the accomplice did not implicate on the first move, Tit for Tat again reciprocated, reinforcing its initial cooperation on every subsequent move.

Most programs were complicated. They strategized, analyzed, and mystified so that their counterpart could not determine their next move. This behavior seemed to elicit ferociously competitive reactions from their accomplices, except for simple Tit for Tat. This Charlie Brown in the field always assumed the best on the first move and then merely echoed its accomplice's most recent decision until the iterations were played out. This strategy often left Tit for Tat Charlie Brown-like, on its back with the wind knocked out of it

on the first move, down twenty to zero. But its subsequent recipro-
cating would, by the end of the twentieth iteration, "elicit cooperation" from the accomplice until some encounters ended in a tie and
most others ended nearly so. The result? Charlie Brown—Tit for
Tat—won the tournament, while all the competing Lucys slinked
home with their footballs.

Axelrod called the successful strategy "eliciting cooperation."
While the losing programs won their individual competitions, they
each forfeited the tournament overall. They looked at each pairing
as an opportunity to compete, to—as Lucy does—leave their accomplice one down. Their tactical ferocity blinded them to a larger
objective: winning the tournament. Tit for Tat, our Charlie Brown,
saw these interactions as opportunities not to compete but to first
cooperate. The best outcome for Tit for Tat would be for each to
minimize the other's cumulative jail time, to never implicate. Others
mistook overall success as simply an accumulation of small wins.
Tit for Tat recognized that ultimate success would require the accumulation of small losses, so it tried, tried, and tried again to elicit
the cooperation that could create this possibility, where everyone
wins the tournament.

Tit for Tat did not succeed in making everyone successful, because its competitors would not allow it. My friend Randy Taylor
recounts the story of a class he took years ago as an employee of
IBM. The class was advertised as being about project management,
and the instructor made sure that each participant left with a book
about project management, but he did not spend any time in the
workshop teaching a prepared curriculum. He instead offered a
series of simulations in which each participant could experience the
destructive effects of his or her own competitive nature. As Randy
recounted it, the instructor, looking out across this roomful of people
who had been specifically hired for their competitive nature, said,
"I want you to understand that competition is a neurosis, and if you
don't learn how to get over it, it will kill you, and this firm along
with you."

Most of our interactions on our projects are iterations of past
interactions, like Charlie Brown and Lucy's interactions. We have
history. In a single-iteration universe, implication becomes the provably
"least worst" strategy. In such a universe, it's always better to

assume that the other one's a snake, too, and minimize your own jail time. But this is not a single-iteration universe. We will encounter, if not this specific Lucy again, another one enough like her to elicit the same feelings, the same memories, perhaps the same nagging hostilities.

HOW BADLY DO YOU WANT THEM TO WIN?

T it for Tat was successful because it wanted its counterparts to win, too. It didn't want to be one-up from anyone. To do this, it had to risk being wrong. It had to risk trusting when trust was unjustified. What was wagered? From the perspective of the individual interaction, everything was wagered. Being down twenty to nothing could be an unrecoverable deficit. From the perspective of the tournament, however, a twenty-to-nothing first-move deficit was merely information, no reason to abandon original intentions. Tit for Tat said, "OK. If that's how you want to play the game—but sooner or later you'll figure out that we're better off cooperating. Will you risk it?" And where the competitor risked cooperation, things improved. Where it did not, both suffered. But the competitor suffered more because it never learned enough to see that in winning the way it did, it forfeited the opportunity to achieve a larger success. Tit for Tat was fine regardless of how its accomplice responded.

So what does this have to do with projects, blind men, and elephant parts? Some members of the community will see everything as a snake, and they might, because of this, be tempted to become snakelike themselves—turning themselves, in this process, into the sorriest sort of safe. Others might acknowledge past experiences and choose to trust—once more, anyway. The project that only sees snakes loses most of its potential and rarely understands the potential it lost at its own hand. What's the real objective, anyway? Taking the flag today or achieving something larger and more long-term?

Sometimes snakes attend my workshops. They seem to enter with that reptilian gleam in their eyes that says to me they're going to be trouble. Some snakes appear to have an interest in proving me wrong or in confirming themselves right; I really don't know their agenda. I imagine worst-case scenarios. If I join the competition, we both lose. They forfeit the opportunity to extract something useful from the experience, and I lose because I steal their opportunity to choose what honestly works for them. Since they can decide the outcome by simply withdrawing, it's in my interest to engage more circumspectly. The question always rises inside me, "How badly do you want them to win?"

A participant in one workshop was disruptive from the earliest minutes. A Turkish Ph.D. manufacturing engineer, he was as politically incorrect as he was very well trained in formal hierarchical command-and-control theory. I was introducing very alien considerations: communities and blind men and elephant analogies, and he responded noisily. One or two participants complained after the class that I should have thrown his disruptive butt out on the first day. Many others, though, said that his resistance was exactly the noise they would have to face when applying the workshop's techniques in their real worlds. They thanked me for staying with him through the class. It took all of my courage to ask this disruptive fellow out to lunch that first day. We had a delightful conversation, which, I later learned, helped him find something useful in the experience. I learned over lunch that he very much appreciated my teaching skills, even though he thought the workshop content was bullshit. Fine enough.

I learned part of this lesson as a teenager, when I worked as a singer/songwriter. When you're onstage, the spotlights obscure from vision, but not from hearing, most of what the audience does. The performer cannot see the audience but can hear it all too well. Missing one sense seems to exaggerate the remaining ones. I learned early on that I couldn't correctly interpret the audience members' experience from the sounds they made. Some of my songs were very quiet and thoughtful. Does an absence of applause mean that they didn't appreciate the reflection or that they didn't want to disrupt the feeling? My choice. I learned that I performed poorly when I interpreted the noises scathingly, as if they were evidence of ill will.

When I could imagine the noises as supportive, I performed better. I guess jerks don't buy folk songs, either.

"I SEE," QUOTH HE, "THE ELEPHANT IS VERY LIKE A SNAKE!"

I feel a bit silly bringing up love in a chapter about snakes, but I have one final point to make. I have noticed in my consulting work that I can't do anyone any good unless I care about him or her. When I have a jerk in my workshop, it becomes my job to find a reason to care about his winning, or I cannot help him. In a way, I cannot myself win without imagining ways in which my fellows might also win. I don't always succeed.

I still sign contracts. My largest clients spend more time administrating their contracts than doing real work, but I don't sign contracts unless I see something juicy in the work for myself and for my clients. I want them to win, too. I have learned that if I have not gone through the exercise of pumping my own belief that this will be a win-win situation, it is very unlikely to be one. Sometimes we have to rely on the contract to come to closure. Mostly, though, the covenant we forge in the dialogue before we ever draft the contract rules the engagement. Whether my client and I decide to trust or to chase snakes always becomes the defining element of that initiating dialogue.

THE TREE

The Fourth reached out an eager hand,
And felt about the knee:
"What most this wondrous beast is like
Is mighty plain," quoth he;
"'Tis clear enough the Elephant
Is very like a tree!"

—From "The Blind Men and the
Elephant," by John Godfrey Saxe

Have you ever listened to yourself as you've prepared your project's plan? If so, you might have heard the voice that was providing the play-by-play commentary asking more questions than you thought you had about planning. Listen between the words. If you're not enjoying the planning, you might be spouting ...

"101 REASONS WHY I CAN'T PLAN YET"

It's 10 o'clock Sunday night. Dinner's long over, and the kids are tucked into bed as most of the rest of the world prepares for sleep. I'm stewing at my desk. Well, I'm not stewing, exactly, I'm

69

more like panicking! I've gone and done it this time! I've committed to getting a plan completed for my project by 10 tomorrow morning, and I haven't gotten any further than to start up my PowerBook and watch the damned incessant, aptly named cursor wink impatiently at me.

I don't have time to do this right. I'm too busy. If they really wanted a quality plan, they'd pull the rest of my responsibilities away from me so I could focus exclusively on putting this thing together. Actually, that might be a reasonable thing to do, except everyone else is too busy to absorb any of my work. In fact, we're all too busy! We don't have any business trying to plan something like this right now. There's just no time!

Besides, I think we're too far behind the curve on this one. We've missed the chance to start the project off right. We should have had this plan weeks ago. I'll bet this phase is close to 90 percent completed now. What good will the plan do at this late date?

Then again, we could be too early. Everybody knows that planning too early is just wasted effort. I'm sure we're missing some key experience or tool that will give us the insight we really need to properly plan this thing. I, for one, could use some more project management training. Can't expect something for nothing—you've just got to invest in training your people. And this PowerBook is clearly not powerful enough to lay out the project plan. I need a faster machine; otherwise I'll just waste half of the time I don't have in the first place waiting for the machine. And this project-planning software is a release behind! I'd better see about getting that upgrade first thing tomorrow. … It's clearly too early to be planning this project!

I'm out of paper clips! And I'm going to need lots of paper clips to get all these planning documents distributed. Is Office World still open? Where are we going to meet to review this plan? I could connect into work and check the conference-room schedule. It's performance-review time; there won't be any conference rooms available until at least the week after next. Not much use creating a plan you can't even review for a couple of weeks! This effort is starting to feel incredibly stupid!

Besides, the most important part of the project isn't slated to start until next summer. We don't need any kind of detail on a schedule until then. What am I doing up at 10:13 p.m. fretting over a plan that doesn't need to be completed until next summer? The project team isn't even assembled yet! We're missing the Architect! I can't plan an effort like this without having an Architect on board!

I've been paying extra-close attention the last few weeks, and I'm convinced that the time is not right for a plan on this project. The group's working pretty well together, but if we get too explicit about roles, responsibilities, and tasks now, we'll upset the informal equilibrium we've worked so hard to attain. Management doesn't understand that sometimes these things are just best left to themselves. Besides, Mondays are especially bad days to roll out a plan. I checked the horoscope this morning, and it said, "Leave the details until later. Enjoy the moment." There has never been a clearer statement of the true situation on this project. If I plan this now, I could kill it! I checked the I Ching. It concurred.

Do I even know how to plan a project? Of course I know how to plan a project, but do I know how to plan *this* type of project? This situation's so unique, I doubt if anybody's ever planned a project like this. Now that I think about it, I'm uncertain if I know enough of the technical details of this project to produce a decent plan. There's probably no use in planning until we get through the discovery process and have a technical architecture to base it upon.

I haven't been in this company that long, and I'm not sure I understand how projects are planned here. All told, I think I almost know enough to plan this project, but not quite. Then again, I'm not sure anyone can ever know enough about this particular project to plan it well. This is R&D, and everyone knows you can't predict a creative process like R&D. Besides, even if I did create a plan, it wouldn't help me manage this thing. I'll have to stay adaptive, no matter what the plan says. The process we're following is quite remarkably simple. I should be able to keep the plan in my head.

Management's been keeping me in the dark about the real intentions behind this project, anyway. My boss has a better handle on the political and organizational ramifications. It would probably be better if he produced the plan, but he's on sabbatical. I get the feeling there are many things I'm not supposed to know about. To be charitable, it may be that my boss just didn't know that I don't know this stuff, whatever it is, when he assigned this work to me. Or maybe management thinks I don't need to know. That's probably it—they're so clueless, they think I don't need to know about all the political issues. I don't know why they're not telling me, but I feel like I'm being set up. The plan will be the target.

I'd like to set the record straight on this project, but I don't have permission. Management is stingy with granting permissions around here. I've asked and asked in the past and been denied authority every time. Well, not exactly every time. I did have hiring and firing authority on one project, but it was taken away from me. I don't know why. Since then, I've asked and been refused. Management should know the authority I need to get their work done, but they don't. Around here, a guy can be denied without even asking!

Still, I do have that as-yet-unapproved proposal that's stuck somewhere in the paperwork cycle. It's waiting on some quarterly evaluation meeting following my boss's return from sabbatical or when hell freezes over, whichever comes first. I've been altogether too busy to follow up, and anyway, the time doesn't feel quite right to be too pushy about this sort of thing. Besides, maybe the biggest problem is that I don't have access to the proper authority to even follow up. I don't know why. This seems like a really inefficient way to run a company. It's awfully hard to get a plan created under this load of bureaucracy!

Why is it always the middle of the night when I realize that my project team has to be involved in creating this plan or they'll never buy into it? Teams around here can be pretty nasty if they feel railroaded into accepting someone else's project plan. They quickly take away a project leader's power if they're not brought in properly. Sometimes, even if you ask, they'll deny you access. Lose their hearts, and their heads will never follow. Makes me uneasy to even ask. But I can't complete the project without a team, and I can't produce a plan without a team, either.

What am I doing here? I clearly can't complete this plan tonight! I know—I'll call in sick tomorrow. That will buy me some time. Maybe the real issue is that I haven't given myself permission to just do what needs to be done to get this plan built. It sounds strange, but maybe I'm getting more from not planning than I could ever get from completing the planning! Could I actually be safer endlessly deferring the planning? OK, I'll admit to a bit of that. Like I said before, I'm not sure the timing is just right, and the timing should be just right.

This project is still speculation, anyway. Yes, some work has begun, but the project hasn't even been formally funded yet. I'm not sure the organization wants to fund this project. If they got a better idea of exactly what this thing is, they might pull the plug altogether. Or they might reassign it to another division. I know they should be more involved, and they will be more involved when the idea is better developed, but bringing them in too early could be a fate worse than death. Not planning will protect this innocent beginning from too many maliciously prying eyes. I'm pretty sure the organization can't afford this project. If we do it without a formally acknowledged plan, they'll have to accept the results. It's the right project to do, whether we can afford to do it this fiscal year or not. On the other hand, I'm not really sure we should be sneaking around behind anyone's back. Maybe if we drag our feet, the organization will quietly cancel the project and my obligation will just go away.

I don't know how I got roped into being responsible for this plan! I don't have anything like the formal power to pull this off, and I can't get it. It's not really my job to do planning—that's a manager's job, and I am not a manager. There's a reason why I didn't go to business school. I'm not the manager type and never was cut out to be. This is just another example of management's delegating the responsibility that actually belongs to them! I'm more of a technician than a leader. There are too many politics involved in a project like this, and if there's one thing I am not and never will be, it's a politician. Let's leave that work to the folks in the yellow power ties and Italian silk suits.

There are rules, laws, and traditions at work here. If I look at who's done this sort of thing in the past, I find a long line of severe punishments. The last person who tried to complete a plan on a project like this one got fired. The one before that got reassigned. I can't remember anyone who tried to pull this off that didn't lose status in the company. I don't remember anyone who wasn't humiliated. Well, at least those were the stories. I haven't ever actually seen anyone get punished, but then nobody's ever managed to get a plan like this accepted.

That's not to say there haven't been threats, however. Management's threatened, team members have threatened, other departments and teams and work groups and individuals have all made various threats in recent weeks. I don't think anyone could please all of these folks.

This boils down to a matter of personal risk. Frankly, my self-esteem feels threatened. This plan will change my role in my work group, and that scares me. My role will change, and I'm pretty successful and pretty comfortable in my present role. My relationships will certainly change, and I'm not convinced that I want them to change. This plan looks like more trouble than it can ever be worth!

I'm starting to sound like I believe it shouldn't be done, or is it that I believe it can't be done?

OK, time for cards on the table. Nobody else is stepping up to this responsibility. Nobody else has had the courage (or stupidity) to volunteer to put together this plan. Nobody except me. I have more power in this situation than I've given myself credit for! If I look at this situation closely, this plan will get done when I say it's going to get done. I may be exposed with this assignment, but anyone else would be even more exposed. I don't think anyone else could even come close to putting this together. Who else could work through the certain punishment, let alone the implied punishment, with no encouragement, to get this plan built? Who else besides me? Nobody!

So I have some power, but I also have some fears. I am afraid of what the plan will tell me. Maybe it will show conclusively that I'm not going to be able to keep up. On the other hand, I'm concerned that the plan will not show all it should show about what's really going on here; we're likely not to get much bang for these considerable bucks. This process of constructing a plan hurts. I don't look forward to that pain. As I said before, I am concerned that others will respond poorly to this plan, and I have no control over their responses. Even then, there's no certainty that the plan will work, anyway. I don't know whether I'm more concerned that the plan won't work or that the plan *will* work. This project isn't going to be a bowl of cherries either way. I'm not even sure I'm up to the task. This is too hard, just too hard …

SELF-TALK

The preceding was the re-created internal dialogue I have when I'm starting a new project plan, and I like to plan projects. I've been pretty successful at it. Even so, I hear these internal voices start through this dialogue every time I face a new project. I don't think I'm unusual in this respect.

I've spoken with many, many project managers and would-be project managers, and most wrestle with similar start-up dialogues. This is the first battle waged in pursuit of a manageable project— the battle with yourself. It is a battle between your worst fears and your best intentions; between the certainty of failure and the uncertainty of any tangible, rewarding success. Success in this internal battle will enable you to participate in more internal and external battles. This will be the first battle you'll wage over this plan, not the last. If you don't win this conflict, you can't participate in the next one or the one after that. Success in other struggles won't be so crucial; this one must be won or the whole project will be lost.

These dialogues haunt me at night, when there's only me, face-to-face with my project. My first experience confuses me. Ineptness follows. Other self-esteem–battering experiences swirl around the central theme of "I can't do this." I fret and fuss and eventually find some jury-rigged toehold in this morass of uncertainty. I think it matters less what the toehold is than that there is the experience of a toehold's being found. A place to start.

There is a myth that a good project manager is a powerful, self-confident human being. This is a myth, although it is sometimes true. I'd rather have a project manager who discovers his confidence by carefully considering the facts and his fears than one who self-confidently swaggers into every ambush. Self-confidence based upon self-discovery by conquering self-doubt is more powerful than self-confidence based upon a decisive disposition. I'd rather start up the hill with some idea of where the enemies are hiding. But this myth persists. And my questioning start-up self-talk sparks unsettling feelings. These feelings interact with my emerging fears to further pull me down. "I shouldn't have these feelings! Good project managers never do." These thoughts prompt another level of emotional response, feelings about these negative feelings, and the mud pit quickly becomes quicksand. I believe there is no practical end to this questioning spiral for me. It will continue as long as I breathe.

I tell myself that there are always a hundred and one reasons why I can't plan my project yet. At first there seem to be more reasons to defer the planning than to start it. This always turns out to be an illusion, but I only learn it was an illusion by planning anyway, in spite of all the good reasons why it wasn't time to plan yet. And I must relearn every time that my reasons for deferring are illusions. In practice, there is no good time to plan. The planning work will always displace more urgent and seemingly more important work. Most planless projects are planless because the project team had more important work to do. As one of my clients told me, "I know we should slow down and decide on a target, but we just don't have the schedule time to do that!" That makes a hundred and two good reasons!

This battle goes to the impractical, to the courageous, to the foolhardy, to the strong-stomached. No one wins this contest by generating a hundred and two good reasons to plan. They win by generating one small, reasonably good reason to plan anyway, and then just getting started. It's impractical to climb this mountain by piling up a slightly taller pile of rocks and then stepping down onto the mountaintop. You climb a mountain by finding the first toehold and then proceeding up from there, recognizing that finding the first toehold is not the end of struggling for toeholds between there and the top. You cannot at the start predict where those toeholds will be or how you'll find them, but having wrestled with and conquered that first, great uncertainty, you can be certain that you've found toeholds before and so you'll probably find them again. The infinite reasons why it's not time to plan are eternal, like the mountain. They will be conquered only one small toehold at a time.

"I THINK THAT I WILL NEVER SEE ..."

How are projects like trees? Trees are hierarchies branching both up and down from a central trunk. We see the trunk or the canopy and recognize a tree without seeing the part of the sustaining organism working silently belowground.

Project organizations are hierarchies that seem to branch only down from a central point. But like trees, project organizations are more complex than they appear. When we see a team pursuing an objective, we recognize a project without ever detecting the invisible networks sustaining it. What soil supports this tree's roots? What nourishes it? What sort of photosynthesis sustains it?

What tree does a blind man see? Perhaps he sees the tree he expects to see, the one that's "supposed" to be there. What tree does a group of blind men see? Does each experience a different one? Do they first experience the tree they last saw together? How do they agree on the nature of the tree before them? How do they organize their individual experiences into a commonly shared one?

The word *organization* suggests a natural order, an organic arrangement. Can I impose a natural order? Just imposing my preference doesn't organize much. Really organizing requires integrating my preference with the existing order and the order I expected to find.

Organization means something different to those organizing than to those being organized. Being organized suggests that some have to follow another's organization, to adopt another's sense of natural order. What about when this imposed order doesn't feel orderly? Both top-down and bottom-up hierarchies seem to be rooted in the belief that someone must lead and others must follow, that some must forgo their natural sense of order and adopt someone else's orderliness so the whole can achieve order. What organizing principle does a tree follow when it branches both up and down? Do the roots defer to the leaves? Does the trunk dictate to the roots?

A tree branches out in an elegantly fragmented order. No two parts are alike. The trunk's order differs from the leaves' order. Both organize differently than the branches, which are ordered entirely unlike the roots. And the roots themselves are not homogeneous.

Their differences range from a trunklike taproot to hairlike tendrils strong enough to crack bedrock. We easily discern oak from fir, cottonwood from pine, and a pair of oak trees from each other, even though every twig remains unique.

My peerless 1950 Webster's Unabridged Dictionary defines *tree* as "A woody perennial plant having a single main axis or stem (trunk), commonly exceeding 10 feet in height." Not terribly descriptive. But how much more descriptive could it be and describe a tree? I think that I shall never see anything half as ambiguous as a tree. Colloquial definitions bring some depth and some more ambiguity to our standard definition: A tree might also be a gallows (a "hanging tree"), a crazy-making experience ("You drive me up a tree"), or a trap ("We treed the raccoon").

What sort of tree will your project be? How should you order the effort? Should you impose an order or let nature dictate form? Should this tree be upside-down or two-trunked? Whatever organization you embrace might become the supporting spindle of your project or the gallows upon which it swings. It might become the thing that makes you crazy or the trap making you unwary prey. This chapter considers your project's natural order, contrasts it with the idea of imposed order, and examines issues surrounding creating effective project organizations.

THERE'S NO SUCH THING AS A PROJECT

A tree cannot see its forest, and a forest cannot see its trees. Any tree in the forest might feel as though its location gives it a unique perspective on the rest of the forest, but each tree sees a different forest from what any other tree sees. And so, no tree "in the forest" can see "the forest." Each can only see "its forest," the one observable from where it is rooted. For the trees in any forest, there are as many forests as there are trees. Each tree has its own perspective on its forest.

Likewise, the forest cannot see its own trees. Since "all trees in the forest" includes the forest, something more distant must see the trees in the forest. Just as you cannot see all of you while being you, because some of what's seeing has to be seen, too, the forest cannot see its trees.

Projects have this same feature. Just as there can be no objectively verifiable entity called a "forest" for any of the trees within a forest, there can be no objectively verifiable entity called a "project" for the individuals within a project.

There can be no such thing as a project.

This first principle of project life remains anything but obvious for most. If I ask you to put your project into a wheelbarrow, what would you put into the wheelbarrow? If you put the plan in there, you've made the same mistake as someone who eats her menu for supper. If you put the project's product into the wheelbarrow, you make the same mistake as someone who mistakes the satisfaction for the dinner. The satisfaction just shows that a meal took place. If you put relationships and intentions into the wheelbarrow, you're getting closer to the point. But what have you placed in that wheelbarrow, really? Whatever you placed there was never a thing! Hence my assertion that there can be no such thing as a project.

UNAVOIDABLE BLIND SPOTS

Our conceptions get us into predictable trouble. Early scientists used to postulate the presence of something called a *homunculus*. They believed this was a physical entity, "a little man" located in the brain, who oversaw all the operations of the brain and body. When someone asked what served as homunculus to the homunculus, the quandary began.

A smart-aleck journalist once attempted to trap Gandhi in a religious paradox. "I understand," he began, "that the followers of your religion believe that the universe is supported on the backs of four enormous white elephants. Is this true?"

"Quite so," replied Gandhi.

"If this is true," continued the journalist, "what are the elephants standing on?"

"Four more elephants," smiled Gandhi.

"And those?" persisted the journalist.

"I see where this is going," said Gandhi, "and I will save us both some trouble. They are elephants all the way down!"

Leaders are easily trapped within this dilemma. Their job overseeing an organization of which they are also a part requires them to find some point that allows them to objectively see the organization they are observing. When I'm observing myself, I cannot observe the part that's doing the observing. This leaves some elements unseen and therefore unknowable. We each have unavoidable blind spots.

IMPOSING DISORGANIZATION

Your organization will insist upon your project's disorganization. It will accomplish this by imposing an inappropriate organization on the project. It will do this because organizations always emulate their products with their projects. They emulate their products with their projects innocently, because they know this form of organization. It seems most orderly to them. Banks insist upon organizing their projects as if they were managing accounts. Insurance companies insist upon organizing their projects as if they were underwriting risks. Manufacturing companies expect their projects to operate like predictable little manufacturing plants. Software companies create projects in the image of their software. Each insists upon a specific organization even though that organization is almost always poorly suited for its projects.

The sponsoring organization does not choose these impositions. It feels impelled to follow them. Organizing projects any other way seems unconscionable. It imposes its order in the same way that your great-aunt might impose a wholly inappropriate Christmas gift. Out of respect and obligation, you show unusual interest in it only as long as she watches. She never learns that pink really isn't your favorite color for a teddy bear. Whenever she returns, that toy reappears from the bottom of the toy chest, featured only as long as she stays.

I wouldn't call this disorganization a problem, because I'd rather think of it as a typical feature of normal project life. I think of it as a feature because attempting to fix it usually creates something much worse.

One project assignment back at the insurance company had me leading a planning project. The purpose of it was to create a project plan for the conversion of a massive and archaic mainframe system (all twelve subsystems of it) to a new computing platform. The organization had not decided which platform. They wanted to know how much such a conversion might cost before deciding such details. Several specialists, a manager or two, a technician or two, and I, cast as the systems project leader (another had the role of "user project leader" for the effort), met two or three afternoons each week for about six months, working to create this plan. We had our methodology manuals—a bookshelf full of loose-leaf binders, each outlining the standard user and technical tasks associated with each significant systems development activity. We followed these books even though we were not by strict definition building anything. We were converting something, which more closely resembles remodeling than scratch construction. Our sponsoring organization wanted this remodeling work done right, so they expected us to follow the methodology's new-development direction, even though it described how to do something we were not going to do. All organizations impose similar contradictions on their projects.

We survived. We knew that our activities were absurd. How could we not know? I remember planning the conversion of the fifth subsystem into that unknown context. The methodology manual for the design subphase outlined the tasks associated with creating reports for a typical software application. The number and complexity of reports depended enormously upon many context details, which we couldn't know.

"How many reports will this subsystem have?" I remember asking.

Specialists, technicians, and a manager huddled and asked each other, "How many reports does the current subsystem have?"

Someone disappeared to gather additional information, returning with some fuzziness, such as, "The standard current subsystem has thirty reports. We created eighteen unique ones to compensate for reports not provided in the base system and disabled ten of the standard reports because they were for stock companies."

"So," I remember saying as leader, "how many reports will the new subsystem need, and how difficult will each be to design?"

After much discussion, we agreed on some compromise number. Then we explicitly assumed relative complexities for each report, and we projected baseline skill-level requirements and task estimates for the activities supporting the design of each report. We had already completed this dance for the feasibility and analysis subphases, and we would repeat it for construction, testing, integration, and implementation. We created in the process a huge loose-leaf binder, a true idiot stepchild of the inappropriate methodology, which held a detailed task-level plan. This plan pretended to show in exquisite detail all of the activities needed to convert the present twelve- headed system into a new and unknown computing platform (the irony was not lost on us, either).

This plan was complete fantasy, but it served the purpose for which it was intended. What purpose was intended? To preserve the organization's sense of organization, of course. This several-months-long planning exercise was approached as if we were underwriting a very great risk—as if we were assessing the insurability of the effort, which in some ways we were. We were not project planners designing a project, but underwriters, actuaries, and claims managers assessing a proposed risk.

The members of the executive committee received our painstakingly produced plan and, each turning to the last page in his custom-made loose-leaf binder, voted unanimously against funding the effort. This was the end of our six-month project to plan the project and the end of the idea that there would be a follow-on conversion project. I'd seen this same group argue for weeks over the fifth-year tax-rate assumption of a cost/benefit analysis associated with a project plan created in the same way as we created our conversion plan.

Why did they do this? Because this is how insurance managers manage. This behavior constitutes good management to them. What did our conversion project have to do with insurance? Nothing, aside from the fact that we were planning the forward conversion of an insurance administration application. The project team would issue no policies, collect no premiums, compensate no agents, stockpile no reserves, and assess no claims, yet we were managing as if we were an insurance operation. Our sponsoring organization insisted upon that approach.

Is this insanity? Perhaps, but the relative sanity of these behaviors wasn't the point. If you work on projects for a bank, you might notice similarly absurd imposed imperatives. If you work for a dotcom start-up, you will notice that it insists upon not the most effective or efficient organization for your project but the most familiar one. Manufacturing companies expect their projects to unfold like repeatable manufacturing processes, and management intervenes as if any project were in trouble should it exhibit any evidence of becoming unpredictable. Engineering organizations impose inappropriate process expectations. All organizations insist upon managing their projects as if these projects were their products. They rarely are.

There are a variety of strategies that individuals within your project community might adopt to cope with such organizational encumbrances. Some of these strategies look like the strategies that anarchists embrace when undermining an oligarchy. Blowing up the opposing blind men won't ensure a better elephant. Neither will vilifying them. How we choose to cope with this universal (dis)organizing feature of project life will influence our personal experience on our projects. If we choose to cope by trying to undermine the ruling oligarchy, we might be unconsciously undermining our opportunities for meaningful success, too.

HOW WORK REALLY GETS DONE

Like everyone else, I learned most about how work really gets done by watching my parents. This probably makes my understanding different from your understanding, but maybe not. My father worked for more than thirty years as a postal clerk. I watched him. Being a postal clerk was clearly no picnic. He had bosses: suspicious, clueless, occasionally cruel, rarely kind. There were coworkers with work styles ranging from overt slacker to obsessive-compulsive. There were patrons, each with specific and subtly communicated needs. There was also an organization, imposed and enforced by management, that ensured that each constituency was poorly served.

My father was one hell of a worker. Give him a target and he got there. He survived the Depression, honing his will on a thousand challenges there. He brought this focus with him when he joined the post office. But the post office was not organized to use his greatest abilities. It had rules, policies, and procedures meant to subvert slackers and freethinkers. Creative solutions were never appreciated. Selfless effort was encouraged but not rewarded. The overall message reeked containment. It said, "Just Keep The Lid On It." His stories, entertaining from this distance, are spiced with a tang of disappointment. The white-lab-coated experts from Seattle angered the town's small-business people by mandating that the post office didn't need to open its doors earlier than other businesses opened theirs. But if the post office wasn't open early, who would be able to fetch the mail after the shops opened up? A cigar-smoking efficiency expert watched from the rafters as if no one could smell his smoke from the smoke-free sorting stations. Work continued in spite of, not because of, management's disruptive presence.

My father recalls that those who worked Sunday mornings figured out how to smuggle doughnuts, which were strictly forbidden at the sorting stations, into the sorting room, without any of the expert overseers ever figuring out how they did this. I learned that work was about smuggling doughnuts into the sorting room.

His stories describe good people trying to do a decent day's work in spite of their management. They resonated back to me as I began to find myself cast in the role of potential overseer. I wanted to at least enable the power that could figure out how to smuggle doughnuts into the gulag. This, I decided, was a worthwhile management objective!

My father's stories about undermining the system to make the system work sparkle with a real sense of adventure and joy. He was the best of all workers, one who insisted upon satisfying the intention even when it meant violating the rule. He was, like many excellent workers before him, misunderstood, and those misunderstandings still catch in his throat when his stories spill out. I've learned in the years since that most people pursue their work with the same tenacity with which he pursued his work. Few slack off in the real world. People prefer doing meaningful work, and we have the capacity to make almost any work meaningful. The post office had a nearly overwhelming capacity for eradicating meaning from its workplace, but even under this overbearing presence, the workers smuggled in meaning and a workable organization the way they smuggled doughnuts into the sorting room. They kept their sanity this way, while getting the "real" work done.

My father is one of the most capable people I've ever met. He was the master of the universe at home and a usual suspect at work. Nothing about his capability or intention changed when he went to work. He kept his sanity at work by focusing upon what his effort was getting him. It bought him a home where he could be the master of his own universe. He used the job as a medium for acquiring this. His trade put the insanity into its place. Nothing made the craziness disappear, but putting it into its place made it manageable for him.

I have found few exceptions to my belief that people are trying to do the best job they can imagine at all times. I think it was Frederick Winslow Taylor again, our self-proclaimed Father of Scientific Management, who claimed that management carried the responsibility to ensure that workers didn't slack off. (He had some curious definitions of slacking off, too.) Poor work most often results from poor imagination, the inability to imagine a better way to work. My clients and my project teams all occasionally suffer from this myopia. My primary value as a consultant or a project leader always comes from helping people imagine better ways of working together. Everything's impossible until imagined.

CENTRAL ORGANIZING PRINCIPLE

Until a project discovers some central organizing principle, community effort seems unprincipled. The most robust centrally organizing principles are not imposed. Because order emerges almost automatically from any community, the leader remains eternally challenged to guide the organizing in such a way that an ordering organizing principle can emerge, whatever the background mess surrounding the project.

I designed a workshop simulation that clearly demonstrates how a project discovers its central organizing principles. Planning is really just a sorting process. When planning, we sort tasks into meaningful sequences to guide our future activities. The meanings we project onto our task definitions complicate the sorting job. We each associate different classes and types when sorting through task definitions. How do we agree on an organizing principle?

Enter the cookbook, the methodology. Methodologies are predefined organization structures. They are the preplanned steps between your bright idea and your project's product. These instruction manuals suggest how work might be "broken down," or organized, to achieve an end result. Methodologies vary in detail and perspective. At best they serve as points of departure, places to start thinking about organization, rarely places to end up after thinking about it. Methodologies are too often imposed as method, as if they were process definitions (and some claim to be process definitions, so more than just misapplication confuses the chef).

Methodologies are useless for discovering centrally organizing principles. How does this organizing get done? My simulation shows how organizing really happens: I split the workshop into two groups. I direct each group to gather around a table. I then give each team a large bag filled with shapes. Some of the bags have simple geometric forms—squares, rectangles, triangles, parallelograms—in a variety of colors. Another bag has multicolored plastic letters. Others have random selections of little rubber figures, miniature tools, or plastic soldiers and animals. After giving each team a bag of shapes, I ask the team members to arrange the bag's contents into the most efficient form possible. Sometimes I give the teams identical shapes. Often, though, I give the teams different shapes. When someone asks what I mean by "efficient," I respond that "efficient" in this context means "well adapted to what comes next." What comes next? "As in a real project," I explain, "we can never know. Make necessary assumptions, and arrange the shapes so they will be easily adaptable to a purpose you assume but cannot yet know."

I deliberately avoid bounding this exercise with any time constraint. Each team has all the time in the world to complete its assignment, yet assigning this problem always initiates a frantic search for order. Some teams cohere around the assignment. Others splinter. Few individuals are able to dispassionately sit back and consider alternative arrangements. Most, by some invisible process, rush to a preliminarily satisfying order. Many explain later that they experienced extreme disorientation, and some even report having felt physically ill, until an order was found. Some team members are trampled by others' dash to order. Some withdraw from this land rush, while others take extreme, bullying charge. A rough order always results from this disorder.

I then ask each team to look at the other team's arrangement and explain the centrally organizing principle. Where the shapes have inherent meaning, as in the case of alphabet letters, the team quickly identifies several levels of organization. Where the shapes are less inherently meaningful, the observing team struggles to describe an organizing principle, but it always succeeds in describing one. Both teams more easily identify subtle disorder, divergences from their notion of how the pieces should fit together. The green letters are slanted differently from the yellow ones, for instance, and the observing team explains this phenomenon in great detail. The observing team always describes a central principle of its counterpart's organization, but its explanation rarely matches the organizing team's intended order. Even when the explanations match, the stories explaining the details diverge.

This simulation revisits an old lesson in a memorable way. If you're not involved in the organizing, you will never fully comprehend the intended organizing principle. The organizers might correct your misconceptions, but they cannot re-create the organizing experience for anyone not involved in the arranging. I was shocked to recognize, the first time I assigned this simulation, how much about understanding order was simply a matter of being a part of the discovery of the order. Centrally planned economies invariably create a tenacious disorder by excluding from the organizing effort the ones who must most deeply understand the organizing principle. Even those who just watch the physical manipulating of the pieces in the sorting effort understand the ordering better than those who are absent. They might not agree with it, but something very subtle and very "sticky" happens to everyone involved in the sorting.

This simulation demonstrates why participating in the planning is always more important than the form of the resulting plan.

Individuals are often offended at the other team's inability to see the organization that seems so obvious and so clever to them. Team members usually say they're glad they're not on that wacky, disorganized operation across the room. Each team sees deep meanings in the order (and disorder) it finds in the other team's results. It sees evidence of the effectiveness of the teamwork that created the organization. The most orderly-looking organizations are often the product of one domineering team member, yet the observing team usually reports that the other team must have had a high degree of teamwork and cooperation to create such an orderly outcome. The most orderly organizations are more often evidence of a strong hand, if not an iron fist, on the team.

I introduce a second round of sorting, the unforeseeable next event I mentioned in the first round. I give each team another bag of shapes, asking the members to integrate these shapes into their original organization in the most effective way. This round simulates a typical replanning exercise, initiated after an original plan falls apart in practice. Teams in this round rarely redesign their original organization, no matter how poorly suited that order becomes when integrating the new shapes. The new shapes are kludged on, and the story about how they fit becomes ever richer. The second round of observers describe the primary organizing principle in ever richer stories. I am always amazed at the coherence of these stories explaining the new organization.

I initiate the third round by asking the two teams to integrate their organizations, to merge. This starts a tangled dance. Whose order will prevail? The most interesting integration happened at a company in the middle of a merger. The teams wrestled with the assignment, selecting representatives from each team to meet in neutral territory to negotiate the terms and conditions of the uniting. While the negotiators were out of the room, one team member gathered the name tents from around the room and taped them together to create a bridge between the two sorting tables. She then declared the merger complete, even though the order on each table was unaffected in the merger. (This was remarkably similar to the real merging events going on outside the training room door.) When the negotiators returned with their centrally planned strategy for merging, they found the two teams satisfied that their work was complete. Surprise! The negotiators couldn't see an order in the one created in their absence, so they persuaded the two teams to reconsider their merged organization. When they agreed to try to "really merge," the woman who created the name-tent bridge stormed out of the room.

Another group effected the merger when a member of one team, upon hearing the assignment, walked across the room and scooped up the *other* team's shapes, bringing them to his table, where he and some teammates integrated them into his team's existing order while the other team's members watched, openmouthed and unbelieving.

The best final organizations have been the products of teams that managed to bust their earlier conception of order as increasing variety arrived. The most poorly adapted final organizations have been the products of teams that tenaciously defended their original organizing principle, no matter what. Said another way, organizing requires unlearning, which first feels disorganizing. Adapting requires letting go. These are not easily satisfied responsibilities. I think we are naturally disposed to quickly sort out chaotic situations. This serves us well when we're threatened by conditions that require us to find a quick way out of chaos. But where we are building more permanent responses to a threat, we're most likely to settle for a shack when we need sturdier digs.

Once a team imprints on an order, though, that order sticks. Those not involved in the ordering will always remain somewhat clueless about how the chosen order fits together. Planning usually dispatches disorder quickly because the ambiguity in it feels uncomfortable. We often embrace a quickly palliating organization when a more painstaking design would better serve us. If we cannot defer our satisfaction, it seems, we might be satisfied with, but poorly served by, our planning results.

"'TIS CLEAR ENOUGH THE ELEPHANT IS VERY LIKE A TREE!"

The greatest barrier to creating project organizations well adapted to their situations never was the naturally disordering impositions of their sponsoring organizations. Nor are the unresolvable perspectives of a project's community members likely to block the way. Our impatience with the ordering process will always be the strongest barrier to robust order. Our reluctance to sit in the middle of the mess long enough to understand and come to some agreement about its nature before responding to it remains our greatest enemy when planning. Our urgent need for order seems at the root of our projects' continuing disorder.

The planning is everything, and the plan itself, nothing. What we do with our sense of disorder when planning is always more important than whatever order emerges from the planning process. Circumstances will have their way with your plan. However well adapted it starts out being, it will crumble over time and require another and then another disordered search for order.

Many say they are reluctant to bring together a potentially contentious community for planning. All of the chaos I describe in the shape-sorting exercise will certainly emerge in the process of ordering any significant project. Good plans are not necessarily the result of orderly methods, and our insistence upon orderly, uncontentious interaction encourages accommodation or despotism rather than robust order. Passion contributes planning's most useful but also messiest and most upsetting ingredient.

Consider bringing the community together anyway. Defer organizing until you're clear about the purpose, the objective, the context, and the inhibiting edges around the effort. Until you converge these understandings, your orderings will clash and your solutions will stumble in execution. No one forges these understandings in an hour here or there. Create the focus of an unreasonable-seeming few days' effort. When plans must be completed without a period of potentially contentious cohabitation, the resulting organization will at best serve as an ideal. Since no project organization is ideally suited to its conditions, ideal plans, like the definition of a tree, are not very useful in practice.

A LOGGER'S TALE

Several years ago I accompanied my father-in-law, a retired forester, on a visit to his southern Oregon property. Several weeks before this visit, he had hired two loggers to clear out brush and smaller trees to reduce the fire hazard on his land. These loggers had left a larger mess than had existed before they arrived. On this morning, he was meeting with two loggers who specialized in cleaning up the messes made by less scrupulous woodsmen.

I sat on a log, conversing with one of the loggers as his partner surveyed the damage with my father-in-law. "When I was a young man," the logger began, "much of this part of the country was still virgin forest. I spent my first years logging in pristine, beautiful surroundings. I didn't get paid squat, but I got to work in beautiful surroundings. Since they've closed down the virgin tracts, I've had to shift to working in conditions like these, where someone has come in before me and trashed the place. I'm more like a garbage man now than a logger. Interesting thing is, though, I'm paid handsomely now. In fact," he continued, "I'll bet your garbage man makes more money than you do. Don't forget this," he concluded, "there's no end to the gratitude people will pay to someone who will make their garbage disappear."

Organizing is like making garbage disappear, and planners are the sanitation engineers of the project world. They transform chaos into tidier forms. No one can remove this trash for you or your community—we cannot pay someone else to make these unsettling messes disappear and hope to create anything coherent to those not involved in dealing with the unsettling mess. We each must don coveralls and haul some trash. We should never mistake the necessary messiness of this work for a poor result. Great order can emerge if we can tolerate the tangled path from here to there.

The resulting organization will be the center of your project—the canopy above, the roots spreading below, and the firm trunk in between. More important than the resulting plan, though, will be the coherence uncovered in creating the organization. The messier the organizing effort, the more those involved feel, at the end, that they could accomplish anything together. Tidy rearranging leaves no one feeling particularly powerful. Much of the sustaining organization will remain invisible to any but the blind men involved in resolving the unavoidable mess and creating the tenuous order. They alone will see the tree.

Listen to yourself every time you participate in creating another project plan. Expect to hear the voice that's providing the play-by-play commentary asking more questions than you thought you had about planning. Listen between the words and ask yourself, Am I enjoying this experience? If you say no, will you enjoy the product of this experience? That's another question altogether. Your organizing dilemma might be most succinctly stated like this: Those who can tolerate the mess receive a reprieve from it, while incoherence eternally stalks those who try to flee.

THE FAN

The Fifth, who chanced to touch the ear,

Said: "E'en the blindest man

Can tell what this resembles most;

Deny the fact who can,

This marvel of an Elephant

Is very like a fan!"

—From "The Blind Men and the
Elephant," by John Godfrey Saxe

NO ONE IS APATHETIC EXCEPT IN PURSUIT OF SOMEONE ELSE'S GOAL

Can you imagine a more pitiful sight than someone trying to motivate another? I can't. If I'm honest with myself, I have to acknowledge that my motivating efforts have always become rope pushes. Yet volumes have been written on the subject of motivating others. How do you motivate a project team? What motivates community? Is it really your team members' responsibility to rely upon you to motivate them? Can anyone actually motivate another?

Can a project leader fan the embers of commitment into a dedicated, high-performance flame? What if he can't? Must

community members submit to such humiliation, as if they require
the kindly hand of some benevolent parent to goad them into pro-
ductivity? What if they don't?

Maybe dangling carrots are necessary when a project pursues
some truly awful objective. But where a mutually self-interested
community pursues an alluring objective, introducing external motivation seems the equivalent of injecting a fine prosciutto with
artificial additives. Most projects are not pursuing awful objectives.
Many that are pursuing disagreeable goals could redefine their targets into really alluring ones. A better question? "How do we engineer a mutually self-interested effort?" Where someone decides that
motivating techniques are necessary, I've learned, the project probably won't be worth participating in. I usually choose to leave
rather than submit to motivation to resolve the naturally hopeless
feelings I experience when participating in hopeless efforts. These
feelings are simply trying to tell me that I don't belong there.

The energy expended trying to motivate others creates despotic
results. Trying to motivate is a form of bribery. Bribery robs everyone involved. The one receiving the "motivation" forfeits an opportunity to discover her own motivating force. The one motivating
assumes responsibility for something he can never fully satisfy. The
deal leaves everyone poorer. The one bribed ends up in someone's
hip pocket, while the one bribing ends up with a pocketful of
someone else's responsibility. Nobody so engaged wins.

Who initiated the notion that people need to be externally motivated? How can this be the case? Offer someone an opportunity
to pursue a personally alluring objective, and motivation magically
takes care of itself. Offer someone a lot of money to endure some
truly awful experience, and she might agree to tolerate the experience, but her agreement doesn't guarantee motivation, nor does it
guarantee success. Such contracts have no covenant behind them.
They leave only burdening obligations, debts, mortgages, responsibilities most likely to be shuffled through.

Every leader carries this choice. Encourage a death-march effort
by engaging in the easy despotism of motivation—pay, perks, performance bonuses, and the like—or help each find his or her personally compelling objective within the collective effort. These are
complicated choices. Many, spoiled by sour experience, will not

believe that there could be a compelling target for them within the effort. This belief becomes perfectly self-sealing. Many will not know what they want. Trained to see work as a set of necessary accommodations to a Master's authority, many have become as blinded as I was to my own personal authority to use whatever I engage in as a medium for pursuing my own alluring result. Motivating behavior robs its target of its own best reasons for engaging.

I am not arguing against compensation—I think people should be well paid for their efforts. I also believe strongly that those who have mistaken simple compensation for the primary motivating force in their lives have mortgaged away their greatest authority. I might not be the best one to argue these points because I stopped working for money several years ago. This doesn't mean that I refuse payment for my work or that I've become independently wealthy. I often ask my clients what they want to pay me for work because I want them to find real value in the transaction, and frankly, the amount of money they extend to me does nothing to motivate me to do a better or worse job. I give my best no matter what the money compensation because my life works better for me (and for those around me) when I am extending my best effort. I engineer my engagements so that they become opportunities for me to pursue something really alluring to me, and I never have to burden my client to motivate me. I figure that if the client has to motivate as well as compensate me, I'm asking too much from him. How would you feel if, when you visited your dentist, she insisted that you motivate her to do a good job before she'd start drilling? You'd naturally expect her to find her own motivation when working on your teeth. Why should the relationship with your project community members be any different?

FANNING THE FLAME OR STIRRING THE BREEZE?

A leader's proper role cannot be to motivate his community members. How, then, should he use his fan? Fans are useful for pushing around hot air, transforming stifling air into a refreshing breeze. Perhaps the leader could use his fan to bring a freshening breeze into his project's stifling corners. I think project leaders find their best role in helping others find their projects within their project assignments, because projects work best when each community member decides to use her project assignment for pursuing her own alluring goal. If no one is apathetic except in pursuit of someone else's goals, helping others discover their own goals can neatly sidestep the motivation dilemma. It also renders absurd the notion that others need external motivating.

Since many will not believe that there could be an alluring objective within their project assignments, this is not necessarily straightforward work. The project leader might feel himself cast in the role of Tinker Bell, pleading with Peter Pan to believe that he can fly so he can fly. Such convincing easily becomes just another rope push, doomed to fail. How could it be your job to convince anyone else of anything? They'll have to do this critical work for themselves.

How might you help them do this? By pointing out what might not be obvious to them and then letting them take over. People are always trying to tell the truth about themselves. They do this in a variety of verbal and nonverbal ways. These testimonies are not very subtle and require no special mind-reading or body language–translating skills. I can usually get the information I need by observing, believing the information I receive, and then confirming what I conclude. People are not mysterious if you just read their T-shirts.

I can make anyone more mysterious than he really is by believing that he's trying to hide the truth about himself. If he really is trying to hide his truth, it might become my responsibility to uncover it. Then, I cannot believe what I observe because he's obviously trying to distract me from deeper, hidden truths. I can capitalize upon any inconsistency in his behavior to discredit whatever might otherwise appear obvious. I might even openly question the meanings he says he makes of his own experiences, rendering mind reading an essential wrench in the leader's toolbox. This focus only seems doomed to fail. I'm pretty sure that I am not now, nor will I ever be, the Amazing Kreskin. I'm pretty sure you aren't, either.

In an early consulting assignment, my partner asked me to observe a project team meeting. This company was trying to build a viable consumer product even though its background was in building supersecret communications equipment for the National Security Agency. The company took its secrecy seriously. Every prospective employee had to pass a most unusual hiring examination. Each was given a small opaque cube and was asked to determine what was inside the cube without opening it. (The cube's content was a closely held secret, and I never learned what was inside.) Those who could not figure out this puzzle were not hired, so every employee was very skilled at covert communication, which was essentially the company's business. This form of communication extended to absurd lengths. Everyone there seemed to believe that exchanges could never be believed on the face of them. In the course of this meeting, the first that I had attended at the company, the man seated next to me, someone I'd never met before, leaned conspiratorially close and whispered, "What do you suppose he means by that?"

The speaker seemed to me to mean just what he was saying. My neighbor was looking for his "real" meaning. I later learned that this was how all communication worked (I use the term "worked" advisedly here) in this company. All information was first passed through a filter that separated as not true anything that could be directly observed. Then the real meaning of the information was mysteriously divined. Whew!

This company didn't make it. Mind reading undermined its ability to develop consumer products. The NSA had been willing to wait while the "real" product-development process meandered into a deliverable result. The consumer market was less patient. This company second-guessed itself out of a potentially profitable consumer niche.

Some people are trying to hide their truth, but few are very good at the deception. Most of us, when trying to cover up how we really feel or what we really think, mismatch our words and our music, muddling our attempts to coherently communicate. This tangle discloses our truth. Every word and music mismatch cues the question, "What does this mismatch mean?" When the words and the music match, the meaning stands obvious, just as the T-shirt says. But even in the instances where words and meaning so obviously match, stating the obvious confirms your interpretation and safeguards against misinterpretation.

You never need to read anyone's mind but your own. Reading your own mind can be challenge enough. Once you get really good at reading your own mind, you might consider helping another get better at reading his or her own mind, too. Here's how.

THREE-PART CONVERSATION

Pay attention when presenting your project idea. Offering opportunities for others to participate always creates potential for you, your project, and your project-community member. While you are busy pitching her role on your project, listen to what she passes back to you. You will usually hear a mixture of complaints, concerns, and reassurances. Each of these comments carries useful potential.

How might your project help her achieve what she finds personally attractive? How do you know that you've uncovered something personally attractive to her? Follow the energy. Prospective project-community members often complain that they do not have time to participate. Hearing this complaint might send you away fussing about being underresourced, but be careful not to get too far ahead of yourself. When these stifling comments arrive, use your fan to create some refreshing breeze. Ask yourself, "How might her participating on this project give her more time?"

There's real magic in just acknowledging her desire. Once acknowledged, it can be addressed. This lack of awareness of what she wants for herself from the assignment usually becomes the biggest barrier to her finding her project within her project assignment. In my experience, she will tell you what she wants within the first ten minutes of the conversation. Attend to this information. You are observing something that, when acknowledged, can become an alluring personal objective for your community member. Finding that alluring objective requires only that you pay attention, follow the energy, and confirm what you see.

Here's a sample of a typical such interaction.

FANNING FLAMES

I enter the cubicle of the data architect who has been assigned to my latest project. I notice a lot of clutter, and because I'm a clutterer, too, I feel right at home. I watch the architect rearranging piles of paper and reassure him that his office looks tidier than mine.

He explains that he's overloaded with work and can't imagine how he'll be able to help on my project, even though he's been assigned responsibility.

I recount the old adage that a tidy office is evidence of a weak mind, and we both chuckle as we shake hands. I describe my understanding of the project's vision, explaining briefly where the idea for the project originated and outlining the project's grand purpose. I encourage questions and openly acknowledge how many components are still uncertain. After all, the project's just getting started.

Our conversation takes us on a brief bird walk to reminisce about some past project start-up experiences. I introduce my idea of how data architecture might fit into the project and then stop, waiting for a reaction.

I get one, stronger than I expected. He has loads of energy behind changing the data architect's role on projects. He calls my perspective "a part of the problem." He confides that his advice has often been ignored in the past, resulting in less than fully functional results.

I acknowledge his concerns and state my understanding of his perspective. Yes, he confirms, I have it.

(My mind races. I feel a bit stifled responding to this unexpectedly strong emotional reaction.) I wonder out loud how we might use this project as a means of redefining the data architect's project role.

My counterpart leans toward me and says he's pretty sure that management wouldn't buy in to any significant changes.

(I hear some real energy in his voice. I'm following that energy now.) I acknowledge his concern and persist, asking what it might be like if management did buy in to some significant changes.

He describes with evident passion a scenario that, if properly framed, seems entirely sellable to management.

I tell him this.

He says he isn't sure and discloses that he's not convinced he can trust me.

I ask what happens if we don't succeed.

Same old thing, he concedes.

What if we do succeed?

Significant change!

Can he risk achieving only the same old status quo?

Put this way, he says, he might as well risk it.

We've hatched the start of a productive conspiracy, and we share a warmer handshake as we agree to meet later to better define the next steps.

How much motivating do you suppose I will have to do to keep this community member focused? I've helped him acknowledge the fire that was banked but still smoldering in his belly. I've suggested that he might use this assignment as a medium for getting what he really wants for himself. Why wouldn't he be motivated to pursue what he really wants? Pursuing the objective, not necessarily satisfying it, becomes the primary motivating component of almost every assignment. Achieving the objective could be an additional— and interestingly enough, completely optional—nice-to-have. Who could fail to find the pursuit of his own passion motivating? My greatest challenge is to help him acknowledge that he actually can use this assignment as a medium to get what he wants.

Sometimes I encounter cynics, those people who seem able to stifle any suggestion that they could use this assignment to get what they want. Anyone can freely choose cynicism, and a portion of every project community seems to get more passionate about what they believe they cannot do. This perspective must remain their choice. Requiring that every community member make the "correct choice" steals his or her real choices. As I've suggested before, cynics are often wounded optimists, people who believed some past dream so passionately that their hearts were broken when it didn't come true. Many have sworn to avoid getting hurt like that again, and so they inflict considerable pain on themselves avoiding situations that might hurt them again. Their choice.

Most will stumble over some alluring objective worth pursuing. Many will already know their personal objective and be fully capable of acknowledging it without my or anyone else's help. I like to know what others are pursuing for themselves so I can help. When someone pursues notoriety, and I see that associating with the project might make her more notorious than noteworthy, I want to be able to point this out so that she can find another target for her engagement. I like each community member to know what every other member pursues so that they can help each other get what they want from their project experiences. This, I believe, creates the soul of community. Helping my data architect redefine his role on the project from shuffling servant to active coconspirator out to change the world makes my leadership role more interesting, too. When I have a mutually self-interested community, I can engage in real leadership work while motivation takes care of itself, as it really should.

CREATING A VILLAGE IDIOT

I t's a marvelous piece of synchronicity that the blind man characterizes the ear to be very much like a fan. Listening makes possibilities explicit. Had I simply fled from the data architect's complaining, I would have lost the opportunity to help him find his project within his project assignment. My listening ear acted very much like a motivating fan.

I have one other point to make about motivation. I want you to consider carrying this idea away from your reading and applying it in your real-world practice. When observing a project community member, consider making the most generous possible interpretations of his or her curious behavior.

What makes generosity so important? We cannot really know what goes on inside others. Most of us have an overdeveloped ability to jump to conclusions, usually based upon what their behavior would mean if we did what we see them doing. The old adage says, "We see the world as we are, not as it is." Because we are not others, though, our meanings, our interpretations, are most likely wrong, especially if we ascribe *our* meanings to *their* behavior.

How can you know what another's behavior means? You, as I outlined above, can confirm your interpretation by simply asking. But what if she lies? Well, what if she does lie? It's always her choice to lie or not. Unless she is some kind of sociopath, though, her misrepresentation will be garbled somehow, with mismatching words and music. You might then choose to ask what she meant by that. A dialogue might start. Perhaps it won't. What will her misrepresentation cost you? I think it will almost always cost you less than the price of failing to read her mind.

In my Mastering Projects Workshop, I introduce an exercise in which I ask the class to brainstorm a list of the behaviors exhibited by people who are committed to a project. I've never had a group refuse this assignment, and most groups enthusiastically fill more than a full flip-chart page with responses. Typical entries include

- Punctual
- Passionate
- Gets assignments done on time
- Gets to status meetings on time
- Actively participates in discussions, asks difficult questions
- Talks about uncomfortable things
- Helps others achieve their goals

Every list has some contradictions that are mirror images, both of which are supposed to represent committed behavior. For instance, what if someone is late for a status meeting because he is helping someone else achieve her goal?

I ask the group members, once they've presented their results, to resolve the contradictions by identifying the one or two behaviors that really mean commitment. A tangled discussion begins. While this discussion unfolds, I start, rather noisily, commenting on some apparently important information to one of the participants. (I have spoken with her earlier, asking her to play along.) "There you go again," I say, pointing accusingly.

The first time or two, few show any signs of noticing what I'm doing. Eventually, after a few sharp "There you go again's," someone asks what I'm doing. I explain that I have made an agreement with this person to point out some behavior I noticed she was exhibiting that offends most of the people in the room. When I mentioned my observation to her, my story unfolds, I learned that she was unaware of this behavior. I am pointing it out to her so that she can become more aware and perhaps change it. The list-reducing discussion continues while I persist in commenting on this mysterious behavior. All eyes are on my target, and some speculate on which behavior concerns me so.

The group members eventually begin to connect their struggle to agree on what behaviors mean with my pointing out what their classmate's behavior means. The exercise usually ends with the group members acknowledging that they could never really have discerned commitment by simply observing behavior. They decide that they can't reach agreement on what any of the behaviors "mean." They discover in this exercise that they cannot identify commitment in this way, so they have to set aside their certainty of what any others' behaviors mean. Even though their intuition might suggest a clear interpretation, if they don't somehow confirm their conclusions, their understanding is based on nothing stronger than projective speculation. They discover that they see their world as they are rather than how it is. Huge learning!

But what about the hapless participant to whom I'm subjecting my "There you go again" commentaries? What's happening there? I am demonstrating one effect of projecting our interpretations onto others' behaviors. My accusations are an example of what I call *Village Idioting* behavior.

When someone takes it upon himself to tell you the meaning of your behavior, he is Village Idioting you. I marvel, each time I deploy this exercise, how few "There you go again" iterations it takes to completely undermine my target's judgment. Only you can know the real meaning you intend for your behaviors. Someone else's insisting upon his interpretation as the most correct meaning of your behavior quite naturally leaves you feeling crazy. Because you cannot get access to his judgment, and he insists that you use his judgment as the correct interpreter of your behavior, your own judgment has no role. Buy in to these terms and you become a Village Idiot, dependent upon others to tell you the meaning of your own experience.

This exercise can become shockingly real! One participant approached me the morning after observing this exercise to tell me that he would not be attending the rest of the workshop. He thought I had overstepped the bounds of reasonable facilitation by Village Idioting his fellow participant with my insistent "There you go again's." The target of these accusations had approached me the previous afternoon after class and embraced me, brushing a hint of a tear from her eye. She saw her ex-husband in my Village Idioting behavior, always insisting that he knew best the meanings of her struggling attempts to maintain their relationship.

I include this exercise in my workshop, and I mention it here, because I have been Village Idioted. I'll bet you have been, too. What started my first Villiage Idioting experience? I later learned that my project's sponsor was reading into my behavior what it would mean if she were behaving the way I was behaving. But I wasn't her! She complained to my boss, who initiated some conversations. My boss put me on a short leash, engaging me in a series of coaching and counseling sessions meant to help me understand how destructive my behaviors were and to make me more aware of them so I could avoid showing them.

"There you go again," she'd say, leaving me checking my rearview mirror to see what she had just caught me doing. My infraction was never visible to me there, though. I became a Slave to her pseudosuperior judgment, while my own judgment slowly became worthless. If I hadn't started these conversations as a Village Idiot, I quickly became one under my boss's relentless observations.

I remember making a strong defense at first, only slowly understanding that I was guilty as charged, no matter how brilliant my defense. I remember waking up in the morning during that time and crawling under my bed, curling up into the fetal position, wondering how I would ever survive another day of such brutal mind reading and inept reformation. I finally figured out that my boss and my sponsor wanted me to leave. They didn't want me to succeed, and in fact they were actively, and I believe unconsciously, destroying my ability to redeem myself. My rule now is: If someone casts himself or herself in the role of knowing better than me what's going on inside of me, I leave. I am nobody's Village Idiot. Neither are you. There are no Village Idiots in your community, either. (Even if there were a Village Idiot in your community, it would not be your job to reform him or her.)

So I am justly sensitive to the power I have as leader to enforce my perspective on the other blind men arrayed around our elephant. I have learned to believe what others tell me about themselves, asking clarifying rather than accusing questions when the words and the music seem mismatched.

I remember the story of the project team member who, after the meeting where the leader asked for overtime commitments to respond to increasing difficulties in maintaining schedule progress, left the building and did not return. The leader was first puzzled. Later, as the remaining team wolfed down stale pizza at 10 o'clock that night, he became angry. How could she swear commitment to the new strategy, as all of the team members had done that afternoon, and then abandon the rest of her team to a midnight regretting that they had ever heard of pizza? The team reconvened at 7 the next morning, still absent the member who had left early the day before. Others on the team were privately complaining. At 10 o'clock, the missing member arrived and the leader took her aside. Asked to explain why she had abandoned her commitment, she reminded the leader that she had been scheduled for a root canal the afternoon before and that even though she didn't feel well this morning, she had decided to come in and help out, anyway.

"DENY THE FACT WHO CAN, THIS MARVEL OF AN ELEPHANT IS VERY LIKE A FAN!"

Your team members don't need you to motivate them. Their motivation has to be their responsibility, though you can help them find their projects within their project assignments by listening to their stories and simply pointing out what might not have been very obvious to them. This listening ear can encourage the flame already smoldering inside them.

People are always trying to tell the truth about themselves. The things they do that drive you crazy are probably the things that are keeping them sane. Your efforts to reform them will most likely result in making them crazy to satisfy your own sanity, and this can tear apart even the most well-intentioned communities. When their words and their music don't seem to match, consider initiating a peer-to-peer, adult-to-adult conversation that might help you both see the elephant from each other's perspective. This perspective, which comes only from understanding that you didn't understand, can become the most motivating component of project work.

Motivation emerges from simply acknowledging the obvious. No mind reading required. What is your project within this project assignment?

THE ROPE

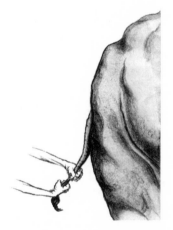

The Sixth no sooner had begun
About the beast to grope,
Than, seizing on the swinging tail
That fell within his scope,
"I see," quoth he, "the Elephant
Is very like a rope!"

—From "The Blind Men and the
Elephant," by John Godfrey Saxe

WILL ROGERS WAS AN ARTIST WITH A ROPE

Will Rogers was an artist with a rope. He could twirl two lassos at once, alternately jumping into and back out of each of them while making witty comments about current events.

I'm no Will Rogers. The only trick I ever accomplished with a rope, as my mother never fails to remind me, was the time I made a lasso and managed to snare my brother around his neck as he rode past the back porch on his bicycle. We both survived.

My grandfather was a cowboy. He used to tell me how a rattlesnake would never cross a hemp rope. He would ring his sleeping blanket with a rope before bedding down at night to keep the snakes out of his bed. He claimed to have awakened one morning to find his rope askew and a snake under the covers. I don't think this story was true, but my grandfather never let the facts get in the way of a good story. Neither did Will Rogers. Still, I'm more like my grandfather than I am like Will Rogers. I'm better at stories than I am at rope tricks.

Ropes can support heavy things. They can tie down loads. They can cordon off. They can also connect people together. Interesting how the same item can keep people out and also connect them together. Mountain climbers stay roped together for safety and to help each other over the inevitable difficult spots. They belay, anchoring in while their companions cross dangerous sections. Mountain climbers rely upon each other, switching roles from lead to anchor and back again as their adventure requires.

What does any of this have to do with project life? I think of project communities as mountain-climbing expeditions. What forms their rope? What connects them together? In this chapter I describe what happens when you give a community enough rope. The old adage says that if you give a man enough rope, he will end up hanging himself. I think the story can be very different for most people, and for most communities, too.

SITTING COMFORTABLY

Sitting comfortably while my client struggles with his learning has to be the most difficult lesson I face in my consulting and teaching career. I can usually imagine myself swooping in and saving him from his struggle, but in the process I would be stealing his most important learning. Only hackers steal their clients' learnings.

I remember facilitating a workshop with another teacher. He was supposed to be observing, but a few times during the week he swooped in to take advantage of what he later called "teachable moments." These moments seemed a lot more teachable for him than learnable for his students. The beatific look on his face as he plunged in to resolve his frustration by "saving" them suggested to me that he was giving himself more from the experience than he was giving to his target—er, student.

I don't withhold my help to be cruel. Allowing people to learn as they learn has to be the greatest gift any leader can give to his community members. Still, the churning feelings I have while watching their struggles are difficult for me to manage. My discomfort with their discomfort echoes through me like thunder down a box canyon.

Some people leave my workshop angry, their experience ringing unresolved in their ears. I'm careful when starting these activities because I know I cannot control how they will play out. The first taste of project community is not necessarily comforting or reassuring. Breaking down barriers might remind us why we built the barriers in the first place. Patience is almost always required. We need the ability to sit long enough with our discomfort in the ambiguity for the coherence to emerge. In this activity, as with so many others in every project, a huge difference emerges between doing well and feeling good about the experience. Those who guide their excursions to maximize the collective comfortable feelings usually end up subverting their true purpose, undermining and eventually destroying their collective adventures.

Connecting with others always dredges up the familiar emotions I first noticed around my family. My family was my first community and the source of my first lessons about how I should behave in a community. I was the middle kid, one of five. I was one of two brothers. My younger siblings were known as "the little girls." I was neither oldest nor youngest. I wasn't the first to try much, but I didn't usually have to bring up the rear, either. I learned that in large families, any kid who didn't need a great deal of attention was appreciated. I learned to get along.

This ability to get along, so valuable for me in my family, became an equally useful strategy as I began engaging in project work. As a leader, I usually assumed the role of provider to my team. I saw my job as seeing that the other team members obtained whatever they needed to get their work done. I played icebreaker, provisioner, and do-gooder. In fulfilling this role, I was like I had been as a kid. I acted as if I didn't need anything for myself. For the longest time, I remained unaware that I carried this role to extremes.

In my conception of my role, I wasn't supposed to need anything for myself. I would do the equivalent of cooking a fine dinner and then declining to sit at the table with those I was feeding. The dangerous part of this role was that it felt so right! Because I was playing a role I had learned from my earliest experiences, I felt literally as if I were back home living in my original skin. I've since learned to recognize such unconscious comfort as a danger sign, when I can recognize anything through this comforting haze. I have to remember to pinch myself occasionally to see if it hurts. If it doesn't hurt, I'm probably in one of those "family trances." When I'm in one of them, I'm running on an autopilot that was programmed for another place and time.

We all do this. And as we lash ourselves together to create our adventuring project community, some in the chain will be there, and some will behave as if they were somewhere else, playing roles designed for another context. Some of these roles will be harmless extensions of earlier learnings meant for similar situations. Others will be wholly inappropriate. Still others might be dangerous under these conditions. Belay systems, those systems of ropes connecting mountain climbers, create friction. Friction stops the fall should anyone stumble. The ropes are also encumbering. They limit movement. They are the overhead cost of a secure passage.

The variety of people and their roles might seem overwhelming. How much easier if we could enforce homogeneity onto this group. Community seems to first try the patience of most of its members. If the community can sit with this discomfort, a stronger connection, a real coherence, can emerge. If the discomfort must be resolved immediately, the coherence will get squashed as certainly as my colleague co-opted our students' workshop learnings. The struggle is never for naught, though, but it usually seems for naught at first.

JUST LIKE THE REAL WORLD

The final simulation in my Mastering Projects Workshop always reinforces these ideas for me. In it, I assign the class responsibility for developing a "bright idea" into a manageable project. The assignment gives the participants an opportunity to practice what we've discussed up to that point, in preparation for deploying their new skills in the real world. Of course I take great pains to create a safe environment within which to do this work. Participation is voluntary. Still, this small simulation quickly becomes just like the real world, as the individuals struggle to become a productive community. I have had only two classes fail to create coherence in this exercise. I have never had a class complete the exercise as the members (or I) originally envisioned completing it.

Where does this real world come from? How does it always manage to encroach into our workshop? One of my colleagues, a Ph.D. scientist, observed another workshop to find out. After the session ended, I asked him. His conclusion explains how the real world creeps into this simulation, too. He said, "The participants bring the magic in with them, but they don't know they are bringing it in."

What happens? Each individual's family trance intrudes. Everyone starts doing what he or she does when he or she doesn't know what to do. This is a reasonable response, because the initiating problem is always ambiguous enough that the exercise starts unformed. As in the shape-sorting planning simulation, some flee toward forming it up as quickly as possible, while others hesitate, sitting in the mud puddle. Each approaches the mess with his or her tool kit filled with the lessons learned from a lifetime of coping with ambiguity. Each brings his or her own strategies for resolving this shared dilemma. For many, the choice of tool seems beyond their personal influence. For these people, the tool finds its way into a hand and starts working before they notice that they're even using a tool. Others make more deliberate choices. How can a community choose when many of its members are blind even to the fact that choices are available to them? This question gets to the heart of building a project's community.

Most communities start as nice-nice groups, with individuals tiptoeing around the presenting problem. Each brings his or her own form of niceness—some withdraw, others take charge, some joke, some follow. This state becomes the background for the first attempt to discover a way around the presenting problem—we'll nice it to death. Sometimes this strategy works. When it works, it usually succeeds when most of the individuals decide that this is not a very important or interesting problem, and so they just let some activist have his or her way. These groups resolve the problem but avoid ever creating a community around it. And for unimportant and uninteresting problems, this strategy works well enough. These successes, however, are characterized as uninspiring experiences by these groups. No one celebrates at these finish lines. Each reports just the residual relief that comes from sidestepping difficult issues.

For the rest of the groups, the nice-niceness erodes into a tug-of-war as the first hints of difference emerge. Some view the problem one way, some see it another. Some easily sidestep this tangle, too, by introducing one of a variety of "group processes."

Many groups employ brainstorming to turn off the apparent churn. The theory of brainstorming works out to be a lot different than the practice of it, though. In theoretical brainstorming, a dispassionate scribe captures all ideas proposed by the group. Ideas are never critiqued. The scribe impartially captures every thought without regard to its apparent usefulness. In theoretical brainstorming, ideas combine to create a synergy in which the result becomes greater than the sum of its parts.

The practice of brainstorming looks more complicated. The scribe has to be drawn from the community. No member of this community can be completely impartial. Some ideas are naturally more attractive than others. Some will try hard to ignore this fact. The scribe always struggles to capture every idea's richness, and the process becomes more focused upon capture than understanding. Abrogation, not synergy, usually results. A good-enough idea gets embraced to stop the churning. Of course, a lot of learning and the potential for coherence stop there, too. But in the face of an unsettling ambiguity, turning off the churn quite easily eclipses any need for a robust result from the effort.

For most, brainstorming quickly falls apart. My best explanation for this disintegration compares what might happen if the six blind men of Indostan, when encountering the elephant, began brainstorming to discover the nature of their shared experience. First of all, one of the blind men would have to abandon his tree or wall or rope or spear or snake to scribe, leaving that part of the experience underrepresented. Then, each blind man would share his unique perspective while the scribe captured every utterance for future reference without commenting or critiquing any of the comments (although questioning for clarity *is* allowed if it doesn't turn into a cross-examination). What do you suppose results under these conditions? Mostly, the frustration escalates until someone "takes charge" and stops the churn. He or she takes charge by either discounting the importance of the problem and thereby making it safe for most to acquiesce, or by asserting his or her perspective so strongly that the others fall back in deference. Neither of these outcomes creates coherence.

COHERENCE EMERGES

For those who stick with it, though, coherence emerges. Sticking with it requires tremendous patience, but this patience is (eventually) rewarded. Sometimes I step in as the Project Management Consultant and suggest a slight change in process. I can best characterize the first hour or two of this real-world simulation as a dialogue of the deaf. Whatever process emerges gets undermined by the unhearing interaction. Each asserts his or her story without hearing (much less understanding) anyone else's. The participants' communication becomes a search to be understood rather than one seeking common understanding.

As the instructor during this time, I get to sit back and watch my carefully crafted workshop crumble around me. Once, while pretending to be lounging in the back of the room during this messy part, I noticed something surprising. I looked at how the participants had arranged themselves around the room. They looked askew, as if some giant had cast them about like so many pick-up sticks. Each was looking in a unique direction. Some stood while others sat. Furniture seemed positioned as if intended to be a physical barrier to agreement. How could a coherent understanding ever emerge from such disorder? I followed my instincts and uncharacteristically intervened.

I asked the group members how they felt about their progress so far. (Finally, a topic they all agreed on.) Each felt lousy about his or her obvious inability to deploy his or her learnings in this silly simulation of the real world. I made an obvious comment and asked a ridiculous question. "Look at how you are each positioned around the room," I directed. "If you found this sort of organization in a mirror, what sort of reflection do you suppose you'd see?"

Silence replied as each surveyed this uneven ground. Someone finally responded, "It would look like a fun-house mirror. The reflection would be unrecognizable."

I suggested a silly something. "Consider getting rid of the tables and arranging the chairs in a circle," I said. "Organize yourselves as if you were a mirror or a lens, with each focusing toward a common center."

Nervous laughter punctuated the activity as they pushed chairs to the side and aligned them into a rough circle.

One participant remained unseated at the end of this reorganization, and she was poised next to a flip chart, pen in hand, waiting to scribe. "Sit down," I told her.

"But I'm the scribe," she insisted.

"I don't think you'll need a scribe for this exercise," I responded. She very reluctantly found a chair as the circle opened to let her join.

"I don't know if this will help," I continued, "but it occurred to me that if I were an idea falling into that organization, I would probably be interpreted in a dozen different ways. Maybe, if we create a common physical focal point, a common cognitive one can emerge, too."

I gave one of the participants a Koosh ball, one of the many toys we bring to our workshop to help people used to continuous action harmlessly burn off their fidgets when locked into a training room. "Everyone gets thirty seconds to state their perspective before they pass the ball to the next person in the line," I instructed. "We will pass the ball around until the popcorn stops popping, until no one has anything else important to say. If you have nothing to say, simply pass the ball to the next person. If you are not testifying, I suggest listening rather than using that time to construct your clever rebuttal. Questions?" There were none.

The blind men began to witness. The blind men started listening. The blind men began to understand that they didn't understand. Each, in his or her thirty seconds, commented on whatever seemed to be the right thing to mention at that moment. Quickly, within a very few minutes, a coherence emerged. What seemed like huge philosophical differences within the incoherent organization seemed like nearly identical perspectives here. Listeners' faces lighted up as they realized that they were, as a community, mostly in raging agreement about the direction and outcome they desired. Once, twice, no more than three times around the mirror and a resolution appeared in the middle of the circle. A common metaphor appeared as if it were an elephant in the center of the room, and each of the blind men easily translated this image into his own dialect. Coherence arrived!

This coherence almost always emerges. I don't know how to engineer it in, but I see strong evidence that satisfying some simple preconditions encourages it to emerge.

ENCOURAGING COHERENCE

Y ou should have caught on by now that I'm not the sort that promotes cookbook strategies for resolving complex situations. Community incoherence is always a complicated challenge. It is also a nearly universal one. The classic strategies for dealing with this apparent collective entropy have always tried to guide the community out of its morass using one of a variety of "leadership techniques." Most of these seem to require that one of the blind men be somehow more aware, more understanding, more enlightened than the others. These strategies discourage real coherence from emerging, providing instead a cheap, homogeneous substitute. The community always has the power to encourage coherence, but no one community member has this special power. How can the members spark this emergent capacity together?

I've watched a pattern surface over dozens of repetitions of this simulation. Sometimes coherence emerges. Sometimes it doesn't emerge. Sometimes it doesn't seem to need to. Where it might occur and it doesn't, several factors almost always influence this result. Looking beneath all these factors highlights six apparent preconditions for encouraging a community's coherence.

Satisfying these preconditions cannot be the community's responsibility, since community emerges from satisfying these conditions. The responsibility lies with each individual, should he or she choose to accept that opportunity. Many have been taught to choose incoherence and the blaming that allows them to focus upon the Masters "responsible" for the mess, and this is always a choice. It need not be a disabling choice for the community as a whole, though. My experience tells me that a single individual's satisfying these preconditions increases the coherence of the group and that even a single individual's coherence can be a powerful factor in creating community. One person can and usually does make the difference.

The communities that become coherent share these factors:

1. They are composed of acknowledged blind men.
2. They share an indescribable elephant.
3. They also share (or have shared) a frustrating experience.
4. They show some patience in the face of their frustration—they stick with it.
5. They make generous interpretations of others' perspectives.
6. Some, although by no means all, also adopt a coherent organization structure; they circle up and focus upon a common point.

1. BLINDNESS

It's not enough simply to be blinded by the situation. Acknowledging the blindness somehow becomes an essential part of coherence's emergence. Some groups expend great effort trying (and invariably failing) to cure the blindness of some of the members. "If only they would open their eyes to see it from *my* perspective," these people seem to say. For these groups, the blindness remains localized and is assumed to be fixable. This apparent localization distracts the problem solvers, enticing them to solve the obvious problem, which rarely turns out to be the defining issue at all. This focus misses the point and usually deepens the churn. After all, if my inclusion in the group has to be dependent upon my being able to see something I cannot confirm from your perspective (which I also cannot confirm), I have every reason to pretend to see it, withdraw, or rebel against your injunction. Incoherence results, regardless.

Embracing blindness doesn't turn out to be either a hopeless or a helpless strategy, but one that properly sets the frame of reference around the situation. Acknowledging the blindness as unfixable means that no one needs to waste time or effort failing to fix it. If I am not responsible for being omniscient, if I can actually discuss my shortcomings, we're all more likely to cohere. If I must posture and pretend, I'm not really showing up in the first place. If I insist that you posture and pretend, too, we are a community of actors rather than a flesh-and-blood community of adaptable humans. We are merely hanging ourselves with our collective rope.

In these ways, acknowledging the community's blindness seems to be a most valuable asset to these groups. Then, at least they can cope with the situation realistically. Frivolous assumptions of superior perspective fall aside, creating a channel where coherence can emerge.

2. ELEPHANT

The community must have an elephant. Complexity often stands in for the elephant. When an objective can only be achieved by bringing together the skills of many different specialties, an elephant arrival can be guaranteed. Where the project's objective can be easily disposed of by a homogeneous set of skills, no one will discover any disagreement in perspective. No elephant can exist there. Furthermore, if real creativity isn't needed to resolve the problem, no elephant can exist. Trivial problems never spawn elephants. But then they don't need community to resolve them.

Any project goal complicated enough to require cross-functional interaction qualifies as an elephant. Some groups are skilled at trivializing complicated problems. Those embracing "best" methodology and process notions always face this risk. Where "all ya gotta do's" abound, an elephant usually lurks unrecognized. Like blindness, the elephant might be attacked as the problem rather than as a statement about the situation. Some ignore their elephant. Others try to simplify the elephant, focusing upon addressing the apparently most important part first. These strategies each deny the obvious and definite presence, and inhibit coherence's emergence.

Until the community accepts the situation as nontrivial, no elephant can appear. No unresolvable conundrum visits. Until the community acknowledges the immensity of the situation, there can be no elephant, and without an elephant, no reason exists for a cross-functional coherence to emerge.

3. FRUSTRATING COMMON EXPERIENCE

Wrestling with accepting the blindness and the elephant often satisfies this criterion. The inevitably incoherent starting activities provide more than ample opportunity for frustrating, patience-trying experiences for the aspiring community. Each member meets the wall. Every community pursuing a novel outcome will at some time before the end of the project hit this wall. Skillful project leaders engineer some wall-encountering experiences as early in the project as possible—not to be cruel but to help satisfy this critical precondition. Less skillful ones tiptoe around acknowledging these barriers.

As I explained above, teams that have not yet cohered into communities might interpret these experiences as evidence that they are on the wrong team pursuing the wrong objective, and in so doing they justify further fragmenting their nascent community. The ones that can, as I have learned to do with my workshop messes, sit comfortably with these unsettling experiences have a better chance for creating real community. I look at these experiences as dedication tests. How badly do I want them to succeed?

For some projects, these frustrating early experiences are evidence only that the wrong team has focused upon the wrong problem. Where these experiences lead to the decision to quit, coherence doesn't emerge this time. Sometimes, though, having shared these difficulties the last time gives the group a head start on its next coherence-building opportunity. When the frustration can be acknowledged, a decision to stop the project and forgo the outcome becomes just as useful as one that agrees to continue as if this were a good idea, even though it doesn't seem to be at the present time. Experiencing a frustrating common experience appears necessary for coherence to emerge.

4. PATIENCE

Whether or not some Master exerts it, teams experiencing time pressure often pursue short-circuiting solutions. In these situations, the obvious lack of headway easily translates into an indictment of the individuals, their processes, or their objectives. Some are more comfortable with ambiguity than are others, but the soon-to-be coherent groups set aside their need for immediate gratification. For these, the difference between doing well and feeling good about the result becomes clear. They appear more accepting of the need to hasten slowly at the beginning than do their clock-watching counterparts. Still, most experience discomfort. They respond to this discomfort not with a lackadaisical nonchalance but with a faith in their collective ability to eventually figure it out.

Project communities always include some who are there to participate in making a cake and others who are only interested in having cake. Those who just want cake easily lose patience with the seemingly irrelevant steps employed by those creating the cake. To those who understand that having cake also means making it, their counterparts' impatience seems unwarranted. This tries the cooks' patience, too.

Coherence needs a gestation period before it can emerge from this collective mess. Where coherence doesn't emerge, the groups seem to fuss and fume throughout this necessary stall. Those that click into coherence exhibit a more patient attitude, reassuring each other that better times are coming.

5. GENEROUS INTERPRETATIONS

When encouraging coherence, listening doesn't seem to be as important as what's heard. The most generous possible interpretation transforms difference from definition into information. The groups that become coherent actively practice generosity. They do not expect perfection, understanding, as Joseph Campbell pointed out, that it is "no place to start" (where would you need to go if you started perfect?) and "no place to go" (because perfection is an unrealistic target!). They interpret each other's struggles not as the cause of difficulty but as potential sources of resolution.

Many of us were raised to be more suspicious than this. Some were told the story of how they need to protect themselves from all those who are out to take advantage of them—they were trained as snake hunters. And there are some out there who see their role as taking advantage of everyone else—real snakes. These people are rare and their influence upon others tiny. Most prefer giving to taking, helping to taking advantage of. Yet so many teams struggle to get airborne on this one point, where no one seems able to interpret anyone else's actions except through his or her personal, self-destructively protective filter.

What have you got to lose by making generous interpretations? Usually less than what you're forfeiting to suspicion. Recovery from generosity punished usually costs far less than the price of sustained suspicion. Cynicism can kill the cause altogether. I try to practice unconditional initial generosity. I can always reciprocate, Tit for Tat–like, by falling back to some defensive position in those rare times when my generosity gets punished. I cannot so easily fill in the divot I create with my suspicious entrée. The groups that find coherence emerging around them all practice generosity. I like to think that the gods reward us with coherence for the faith we show in each other.

6. COHERENT ORGANIZATION

My suggestion that the group members organize themselves into a shape like a mirror or lens might be just a parlor trick. It's a lot easier to pull off in a classroom than in a real-world project situation, but I think we can each mentally circle up and listen, even when we cannot physically arrange ourselves in a circle. The incoherence we personally experience often results from the organization in which we find ourselves immersed. When we're neck-deep in such soup, it shouldn't surprise us that we smell like the soup we're simmering in. We might interpret these incoherences as originating with some individual or subgroup before we ever suspect the context they're in. Often, changing our internal context changes the curious behaviors in the same way that reorganizing the participants in the workshop changed their experience.

Context changes more easily than does group behavior. I'm fiddling with the community's frame of reference here. There are many strategies I might have suggested for helping my workshop group discover coherence, but changing the context seemed easier than changing the people or their beliefs. Changing the context doesn't always yield the desired outcome, but it usually results in some discernible difference. That's more than I can say for most attempts to change behaviors and beliefs.

Sometimes the context, the underlying organization, is unchangeable. As I discussed in Chapter 6, "The Tree," when someone foists an organization upon a project, the resulting incoherences are endemic. Merely acknowledging this fact—that the present context sucks and we're stuck with it—can transform our experiences within the otherwise unchangeable context. Like accepting the blindness and the elephant's complexity, acknowledgment alone seems to help us more coherently cope with the situation.

"I SEE," QUOTH HE, "THE ELEPHANT IS VERY LIKE A ROPE!"

I think it's fitting that this chapter leaves us at the tail of the beast. Having progressed around the animal, we are literally near its end. That we might mistake this ending for a rope seems wonderfully apt. The coherence that ties together our project experience and creates that sense of community is a property more often found nearer the end of an undertaking. Beginnings tend toward incoherence; change initiates chaos. With practice, though, coherence can tie together our common experiences, especially those that start messy.

Coherence, that ability to similarly interpret shared experiences, is not the purpose of any project, yet it amplifies every project's purpose. Project management cannot create the coherence that enables projects to become adaptive and self-managing, but the individuals on any project can devise it. One acting alone can significantly influence its emergence. Several acting together nearly guarantee it.

The old adage reminds us that "we see the world as we are, not as it is." We see the elephant as we are, too. Discovering the elephant can be an act of self-discovery. As our emerging communities remind us, coherence comes to those who can acknowledge their shortcomings in the face of the complexity of their undertakings, to those who share frustrating experiences and are patient with their early awkwardness, and to those who extend generosity in spite of the complicating contexts within which they find themselves. These are deeply human responses to truly difficult conditions. It should not surprise any of us that coherence emerges where our own humanity thrives.

No rope tricks required.

THEOLOGIC WARS

And so these men of Indostan
Disputed loud and long,
Each in his own opinion
Exceeding stiff and strong,
Though each was partly in the right,
And all were in the wrong!

Moral:
So oft in theologic wars,
The disputants, I ween,
Rail on in utter ignorance
Of what each other mean,
And prate about an Elephant
Not one of them has seen!

—From "The Blind Men and the Elephant," by John Godfrey Saxe

A HERETIC'S HOMECOMING

I have spent most of my professional life feeling like a heretic engaged in project theologic wars. I came to this role honestly, as most come to project work. Using my training and experience in operational work, I had organized people, drafted procedures, created metrics, and assessed efficiency. I innocently brought these skills to my project work as if they would be directly applicable. I found a methodology that my peers and I inflicted upon our customers. Our results disappointed all of us.

My partner tells the story of returning from her first project management training to discover that her projects ran worse when she applied the processes she learned there. Later, reflecting on this result, she fell back to applying the techniques she'd learned selling Tupperware, and her project performance improved. She had discarded her most applicable experience when she assumed her new responsibilities. Selling Tupperware taught her the fundamentals of building community, which were exactly applicable to managing a Fortune 100 company's reengineering project. Who would have guessed?

My error, as I reflect back on it now, was of the same order. I went looking for orientation in all the wrong places. I understand that much of what passes for project management process in the world today focuses more on keeping a lid on projects than on opening their true potential. It's as if the whole body of knowledge were based on the assumption that people, left to their own devices, would quite naturally trend toward chaos. Few ideas could be further from my experience.

People create a common rhythm together, not unmanageable chaos. Project an alluring future, and people cohere. They might battle endlessly over differing theories about how to get there, like our blind men around their elephant, but it's their theologies that are in dispute, not their objective. Their individual passion blinds them to their commonality.

We are each expert at being human. We fall into the greatest trouble when we discount this expertise. My first conference presentation introduced a simulation exercise intended to illustrate this principle. I divided the attendees into pairs, one playing the expert and the other his or her customer. I instructed the experts to employ what I called my Peerless Methodology, a failure-proof method for gathering customer requirements. My methodology instructed each expert to hold his customer's hand while looking deeply into her eyes and repeating everything the customer said. After five minutes, the experts and their customers were blood enemies. Left to their own devices as peers, each pair could have found its own way of connecting and communicating. The Peerless method short-circuited this natural ability.

Process can always replace relationship. Process extended to theologic adherence easily displaces our natural abilities to relate with each other. Replacing relationship with process might seem like a very good idea if I believe that people will naturally fall into chaos without it. If I observe, such a notion cannot long persist. The more I experienced the defined and enforced process side of this life, the more of a heretic I became.

By the time you've been in the project business as long as I have, you've experienced at least one extraordinary project, one that keeps you looking for another one to re-create that phenomenal experience. What was that experience, anyway? Ask those of us who have had it, and you'll learn that it had nothing to do with bringing the project in on time, on budget, or on spec. Most of my most remarkable project experiences did not achieve these measures of success, nor would those participating have traded their experience for meeting them.

We experienced on those projects the coherence of a community passionately pursuing a personally meaningful objective. The passionate pursuit and the coherence and the resulting sense of community made the effort meaningful, not meeting the objective or satisfying any external measures of success. Were the customers delighted by the outcome? You bet! Would they have traded away their experience for merely satisfying their original objectives? Not on your life! (And *they* were paying the bills!)

One snootful of this experience and I was a heretic for life. Project management as practiced became pale and absurd. I took up my side of the argument, working to replicate these exquisite experiences of coherence rather than searching for best practice or consistent process.

Now I am coming home. I discovered that I had no argument with the project management professionals, or they with the feral practitioners like me. We pursue the same state—some of us from a mechanical orientation and others from an organic one. The wisest of us pull from many perspectives, not insisting upon one to the exclusion of any others. We can argue endlessly about how our collective coherence emerges, but coherence seems the objective of both the orthodoxy and the heretic.

The coherence we've achieved informs us differently. The process-oriented believe their processes will increase the likelihood of everyone's achieving coherence and community together, while the relationship-oriented ones believe that human adaptation will get us all there. Both are in the right, of course, and all of them are wrong. Not one of us has ever engineered a coherent project, but most of us have experienced one, and even those who have not experienced one aspire to taste one. We each, prating about an elephant not one of us has seen, attribute different causes to this overwhelmingly alluring effect, insisting that others follow our means for achieving what we are all certainly pursuing.

There are many ways to achieve this common end. In fact, there can be no single way for a community to achieve it. If I insist upon following my own means for getting there, then I must extend this same courtesy to you. Otherwise, we perpetuate the simple paradox that someone must accept personal incoherence in order to participate in a coherent community—this becomes the very soul of our theologic wars.

"AND PRATE ABOUT AN ELEPHANT NOT ONE OF THEM HAS SEEN!"

Projects, like companies, never succeed or fail on the goodness of their plans, but judges have only plans to assess results against. So we maintain two sets of books, one for the judges and another for those of us inventing our future. Those who confuse the purpose of their undertaking for these window dressings are simply doomed. Those who engage without being clear about their purpose will certainly lose their way. Those who forget that there are powerful and naive judges watching fare little better. The window dressings do serve a purpose, but they can never be *the* purpose.

There are no "real numbers" in our estimates. You will not find much reality in your objective, your processes for meeting your objective, or even the means you employ for reporting your progress along the way. The interesting fact remains, though, that despite these intangible foundations, we expend real life on our projects.

We make the same investment regardless of the return on our investment, and we are in charge of determining only our return, not the amount invested. When we are unclear about our purpose, we forfeit the only solid point of influence we have over our projects. How would your project be different if you understood that you actually are and always have been the Master in charge?

Several years ago I stopped attending project management conferences. I didn't feel at home there. My presentations received good reviews, but the context seemed alien. To tell you the truth, I felt like a phony there. I hadn't ever been responsible for developing a multibillion-dollar telecommunications technology. In fact, no one has. They didn't complete those projects. Some unacknowledged community did. Those who have pursued these particular elephants could not be wiser or more experienced than I am about myself. They cannot know what I should do. Yet the conferences venerate these poor souls and their contributions, never mentioning the elephant, the pursuit of coherence, which I know was—or if it wasn't, it could have been—the purpose behind their engagements.

I've had it with those, myself included, who make their stock on all they have achieved in this world. I've decided to sponsor a project failure conference, one where participants can share their most discouraging experiences. Those who have not been discouraged by their projects can attend the conference with the shiny-suited consultant crowd. We will present awards for the greatest persistence in the pursuit of coherence, because this is the precondition for real project success. Don't let the Shinola salesmen tell you different.

I recently visited South Dakota with my wife, Amy. Her aunt, Sister Josita, was celebrating fifty years as a Presentation nun, and we planned to attend the Jubilee mass celebrating the event. My father was excommunicated by his parish priest when he married my mother, so I always feel a bit unsettled entering these churches. (I am the offspring of a theologic war!) On this occasion, we were seated immediately behind the visiting clergy, a bishop, and a dozen priests who were related to the celebrating sisters. One priest immediately ahead of me and to my right continually yawned into his prayer-clasped hands. Another just mouthed the words to one hymn, much as I had done in the past. Another sang decidedly off-key. The bishop, in his homily to the sisters, noted that while we were congregated to celebrate their years of dedicated effort, it was not their achievements that would leave the most lasting influence on their many communities. He said it was their dedicated pursuit—their stumbles, their failures, their many falling-short experiences—that were most memorable and instructive to their communities. I reflected on my own experiences and hesitatingly agreed for myself, too.

I hope this book has reassured you that your project experiences can be extraordinary without ever satisfying "how they were supposed to be." How they really were supposed to be must, finally, be how they actually turned out. Our struggles with acknowledging this simple truth linger at the root of many of our most enduring project difficulties. These struggles are completely human, although our attempts to cope with them too often feel altogether inhuman. This feels human, too.

This elephant that not one of us has seen keeps me coming back for more, even though each project brings with it the struggles that come with every collective pursuit.

- Even though I am sure to meet my wall and once again question my intentions for being involved, I come back.
- Even though I will certainly struggle, as if for the first time, with my ethical responsibility to be a bad soldier within an unappreciative bureaucracy, I come back.
- Even though I will find myself wrestling with snakes, painfully learning all over again the self-preserving necessity of trusting and generosity, I come back.
- Even though forests will tangle with trees, and the resulting disorganization will try my patience all over again, I come back.

You see, I might be able to help someone else find his or her project within this project—or someone might be able to help me find my own project there. We have an outside chance, maybe just a tiny chance, to create, again, together, that elephant, that timeless sense of coherence we find whenever we passionately pursue something as a community—so I keep coming back. Don't you?

May this elephant emerge whenever you engage.

MAKE THE BEST

Make the Best
Of the curious choices life gives you.
They won't always rhyme,
And there won't always be a reason behind them.
'Cause this is a sloppy opera and a stupid ballet
And if it isn't for the best, at least it is forever!

So take your time
To know what you're wanting,
What you intend.
Don't go out of your way to avoid what they'll probably say about you anyway.
Even if it were true,
It still couldn't hurt you.
So just move toward the light knowing the rest are right behind you.

And take a hand
From the many, many offered you in your time.
Every inch of your way was meant to be that way
Just for you.
You know we all wear a tutu in this stupid ballet,
And even if it isn't for the best, it never goes away.

So Make the Best,
Take your time,
and take a hand.

—David A. Schmaltz

BIBLIOGRAPHY

. . . .

The following is a list of the author's recommendations for additional reading about project management and related topics. It is also available on the True North Heretics' Forum (http://pc.wiki.net/wiki.cgi ?MasteringProjectsBibliography). There, clicking an ISBN link will take you to Amazon.com, where you may order the book, read reviews, and sample chapters of some of the books.

Adams, James L. *Conceptual Blockbusting: A Guide to Better Ideas.* New York: Cambridge, Mass.: Perseus Books, 2001. ISBN 0738205370. A fundamental work on the subject of thinking yourself out of being stuck.

Axelrod, Robert M. *The Evolution of Cooperation.* New York: Basic Books, 1984. ISBN 0465021220. I reference this book in Chapter 5, "The Snake." Here you'll find the whole story behind Tit for Tat and the iterated Prisoner's Dilemma.

Bayles, David, and Ted Orland. *Art and Fear: Observations on the Perils (and Rewards) of Artmaking.* Santa Barbara, Calif.: Capra Press, 1994. ISBN 0884963799. This book should be in every project participant's bookcase because it covers the one subject no one learns about in school—how to survive as an artist in this world.

Brooks, Frederick P., Jr. *The Mythical Man-Month: Essays on Software Engineering.* Rev. ed. Boston: Addison-Wesley, 1995. ISBN 0201835959. A case study of coherent community.

Carse, James P. *Finite and Infinite Games: A Vision of Life As Play and Possibility.* Reissue ed. New York: Ballantine Books, 1994. ISBN 0345341848. Outlines a powerful way to interpret your experience and engineer your life by adopting a less finite, win/win perspective.

Cashman, Kevin. *Leadership from the Inside Out: Becoming a Leader for Life.* Salt Lake City, Utah: Executive Excellence, 1999. ISBN 1890009318.

Who are you? Where are you going? Why are you going there? A very useful manual for clarifying your purpose here.

DeMarco, Tom. *Structured Analysis and System Specification*. Facsimile ed. Englewood Cliffs, N.J.: Yourdon Press/Prentice Hall, 1985. ISBN 0138543801. A fundamental manual for creating real-world coherent communication.

Dörner, Dietrich, *The Logic of Failure: Recognizing and Avoiding Error in Complex Situations*. Translated by Rita Kimber and Robert Kimber. Cambridge, Mass.: Perseus Books, 1996. ISBN 0201479486. Looks at how people cope with ambiguous situations and provides huge insights into the nature of planning and following those plans.

Elgin, Suzette Haden. *Try to Feel It My Way: New Help for Touch Dominant People and Those Who Care about Them*. New York: John Wiley & Sons, 1996. ISBN 0471006696. A beautiful description of a very different way some people experience and navigate this world.

Fisher, Roger, and Scott Brown. *Getting Together: Building a Relationship That Gets to Yes*. Boston: Houghton Mifflin, 1988. ISBN 0395470994. Continues developing the model into the world of building robust relationships.

Fisher, Roger, and William Ury. *Getting to Yes: Negotiating Agreement without Giving In*. 2nd ed. Boston: Houghton Mifflin, 1992. ISBN 0395317576. This book woke me up when I first read it by offering a workable model for resolving human disagreements.

Gall, John. *Systemantics: The Underground Text of Systems Lore*. New York: Pocket Books, 1986. ISBN 0961825103. The second edition of the 1977 classic *Systemantics: How Systems Work and Especially How They Fail,* revealing how projects actually work. One of the funniest books ever written.

Gause, Donald C., and Gerald M. Weinberg. *Are Your Lights On? How to Figure Out What the Problem Really Is*. New York: Dorset House, 1990. ISBN 0932633161. My friend Jerry Weinberg's delightful guide to sidestepping the difficulties in our lives.

Gilovich, Thomas. *How We Know What Isn't So: The Fallibility of Human Reason in Everyday Life*. New York: The Free Press, 1993. ISBN 0029117062. Just as the title says, this book explains how we decide what isn't true. A handy manual for those who need their certainty threatened.

Gladwell, Malcolm. *The Tipping Point: How Little Things Can Make a Big Difference*. New York: Little, Brown, 2000. ISBN 0316316962. A brilliant description of the invisible influence of context on those swimming through it.

Glass, Robert L. *Computing Calamities: Lessons Learned from Products, Projects, and Companies That Failed*. Englewood Cliffs, N.J.: Prentice Hall, 1998. ISBN 0130828629. Need more reassurance that projects don't happen as planned? Look here.

—————. *Software Runaways: Lessons Learned from Massive Software Project Failures*. Englewood Cliffs, N.J.: Prentice Hall, 1997. ISBN 013673443X. More stories about how projects sometimes don't work at all.

Gracian, Balthasar. *The Art of Worldly Wisdom*. Translated by Joseph Jacobs. Boston: Shambhala Publications, 1993. ISBN 1570627452. This book is five hundred years old and full of timeless wisdom for the practicing politician.

Greenburg, Dan, with Marcia Jacobs. *How to Make Yourself Miserable for the Rest of the Century*. New York: Vintage Books, 1987. ISBN 0394750799. Once you learn the tricks for making yourself miserable, you'll have a nearly impossible time being miserable.

Haley, Jay. *The Power Tactics of Jesus Christ and Other Essays*. 2nd ed. New York: W. W. Norton & Company, 1989. ISBN 0931513057. Strategies for successfully interacting with difficult orthodoxies.

Handy, Charles. *The Age of Paradox*. Boston: Harvard Business School Press, 1989. ISBN 0875844251. Outlines some of the key principles of successfully identifying and coping with paradox, a common feature of project life.

Henderson, Bill. *Tower: Faith, Vertigo, and Amateur Construction*. New York: Farrar, Straus and Giroux, 2000. ISBN 0374278512. Another story of coherent project community.

Hesselbein, Frances, et al., eds. *The Community of the Future*. Reprint ed. The Drucker Foundation Future series. San Francisco: Jossey-Bass, 2000. ISBN 0787952044. A delightful collection of essays about how community happens.

Hofstadter, Douglas R. *Metamagical Themas: Questing for the Essence of Mind and Pattern*. Reissue ed. New York: Bantam Doubleday Dell, 1989. ISBN 0553346830. This is where I first encountered the Prisoner's Dilemma.

Isaacs, William. *Dialogue and the Art of Thinking Together: A Pioneering Approach to Communicating in Business and in Life*. New York: Doubleday, 1999. ISBN 0385479999. Offers a model that explains how deep understanding can be encouraged within your peer-to-peer conversations.

Karten, Naomi. *Managing Expectations: Working with People Who Want More, Better, Faster, Sooner, NOW!* New York: Dorset House, 1994. ISBN 0932633277. An essential addition to everyone's community-building library.

Keirsey, David, and Marilyn Bates. *Please Understand Me: Character and Temperament Types*. 5th ed. Del Mar, Calif.: Prometheus Nemesis Book Company, 1984. ISBN 0960695400. A fine introduction to understanding the different approaches around us.

Kennedy, Eugene, ed., and Sara C. Charles. *On Becoming a Counselor: A Basic Guide for Nonprofessional Counselors*. New expanded ed. New York: Continuum Publishing Group, 1990. ISBN 0826405061. "The things about others that drive you crazy are the things that are keeping them sane." Such golden insights make this an irreplaceable sourcebook for helping ourselves and those around us.

Kerth, Norman L. *Project Retrospectives: A Handbook for Team Reviews*. New York: Dorset House, 2001. ISBN 0932633447. A clear, entertaining description of how we might better learn from our collective experiences.

Kidder, Tracy. *The Soul of a New Machine*. New York: Back Bay Books, 2000. ISBN 0316491977. Another story of how coherent community might emerge.

Kohn, Alfie. *No Contest: The Case Against Competition*. Rev. ed. Boston: Houghton Mifflin, 1992. ISBN 0395631254. A beautiful story explaining how competition destroys possibility.

Leritz, Len. *No-Fault Negotiating: A Simple, Innovative Approach for Solving Problems, Reaching Agreements, and Resolving Conflicts*. Portland, Ore.: Pacifica Press, 1988. ISBN 0961854308. A wonderfully human approach to understanding and working with our differences.

MacKenzie, Gordon. *Orbiting the Giant Hairball: A Corporate Fool's Guide to Surviving with Grace*. New York: Viking Press, 1998. ISBN 0670879835. A completely delightful story of how to survive the corporate life.

Mitchell, Richard. *The Gift of Fire*. North Pomfret, Vt.: Trafalgar Square Books, 2000. ISBN 1888173947. This book has the most remarkable description of learning I have ever encountered. Imagine Prometheus returning to see how we've put his gift of fire to use, only to be presented with a Mensa exam.

Morris, Peter W. G., George H. Hough, and W. G. Morris. *The Anatomy of Major Projects: A Study of the Reality of Project Management*. New York: John Wiley & Sons, 1988. ISBN 0471915513. This classic from scholars at Oxford University describes how major projects don't work as planned.

Myers, Isabel Briggs, with Peter B. Myers. *Gifts Differing: Understanding Personality Type*. Palo Alto, Calif.: Consulting Psychologists Press, 1985. ISBN 089106074X. Background information about yourself and the different behaviors you experience around you. The source work behind the 16 personality types in the Myers-Briggs Type Indicator.

Oshry, Barry. *Seeing Systems: Unlocking the Mysteries of Organizational Life*. San Francisco: Berrett-Koehler, 1996. ISBN 1881052990. Explains how some believe they can see what no blind man can see. Offers some ideas for responding to their certainty.

Perrow, Charles. *Normal Accidents: Living with High-Risk Technologies*. Updated ed. Princeton, N.J.: Princeton University Press, 1999. ISBN 0691004129. Explains why failure is inevitable (but not necessarily catastrophic).

Piattelli-Palmarini, Massimo. *Inevitable Illusions: How Mistakes of Reason Rule Our Minds*. Translated by Keith Botsford. New York: John Wiley & Sons, 1994. ISBN 0471581267. Another handy manual for those who need their certainty poked at.

PMI PMBOK Standards Committee. *A Guide to the Project Management Body of Knowledge (PMBOK Guide)—2000 Edition*. Drexel Hill, Pa.: Project Management Institute, 2001. ISBN 1880410230. A semiridiculous attempt to document the knowledge needed to successfully manage projects. If this premise doesn't amuse you, the execution should. Check out all that's not there, but this is still a useful description of the sorts of window dressing some will insist from you. Remember, this *is* coherence for some of your community members.

Raymond, Eric S. *The Cathedral and the Bazaar: Musings on Linux and Open Source by an Accidental Revolutionary*. Rev. ed. Cambridge, Mass.: O'Reilly & Associates, 2000. ISBN 0596001088. The story of the development of Linux, the operating system that the orthodoxy believed could not be built that way. A modern story of how community creates coherence.

Satir, Virginia. *The New Peoplemaking*. Palo Alto, Calif.: Science and Behavior Books, 1988. ISBN 0831400706. A classic of family therapy. These models are perfectly applicable to your community relationships.

Seligman, Martin E. P. *Learned Optimism: How to Change Your Mind and Your Life*. New York: Pocket Books, 1998. ISBN 0671019112. Essential instruction on explaining your experiences to yourself.

Sher, Gail. *One Continuous Mistake: Four Noble Truths for Writers*. New York: Penguin, 1999. ISBN 0140195874. This book completely reframed my understanding of project work, from one pursuing perfection to "one continuous mistake."

Siu, R. G. H. *The Craft of Power*. Reprint ed. Melbourne, Fla.: Krieger Publishing Company, 1985. ISBN 0898747996. A remarkable work by a Zen master who also happens to be a Washington bureaucrat.

Taylor, Frederick Winslow. *The Principles of Scientific Management*. New York: W. W. Norton & Company, 1967. ISBN 0393003981. Probably the most influential book ever written about management; most of the perspective is useless but nonetheless influential.

Watzlawick, Paul. *The Situation Is Hopeless, but Not Serious: The Pursuit of Unhappiness*. Reprint ed. New York: W. W. Norton & Company, 1993. ISBN 0393310213. A perfect description of project life. How to co-opt your most disappointing experiences.

Watzlawick, Paul, John Weakland, and Richard Fisch, M.D. *Change: Principles of Problem Formation and Problem Resolution*. New York: W. W. Norton & Company, 1988. ISBN 0393011046. A foundational work that first opened my eyes to the possibility of shifting my interpretation of my experience as a means of creating real change.

Weinberg, Gerald M. *Becoming a Technical Leader: An Organic Problem-Solving Approach*. New York: Dorset House, 1986. ISBN 0932633021. Another title from my friend Jerry Weinberg. This one changed my life by offering an organic explanation for how leadership might happen.

Whyte, David. *Crossing the Unknown Sea: Work As a Pilgrimage of Identity*. New York: Riverhead Books, 2001. ISBN 1573221783. A moving story of a man's struggles to take full responsibility for his work and his life.

———. *The Heart Aroused: Poetry and the Preservation of the Soul in Corporate America*. New York: Currency/Doubleday, 1996. ISBN 0385484186. Whyte is a poet who teaches executives how to write poetry.

Wiest, Jerome D., and Ferdinand K. Levy. *A Management Guide to PERT/CPM: With GERT/PDM/DCPM and Other Networks*. Englewood Cliffs, N.J.: Prentice Hall, 1977. ISBN 0135491053. Written by those most responsible for the wide acceptance of automated scheduling tools, this book explains why none of them work. (The algorithm within them was designed to work only in a very narrow, virtually never encountered set of situations.)

INDEX

· ·

ABOUT THE AUTHOR

DAVID A. SCHMALTZ had no idea what he was getting into when he volunteered to help clean up the mess following a bungled computer system conversion back in the '70s. He found that his background as a freelance singer-songwriter and a pot washer prepared him well for the realities of project work. While helping to clean up the conversion mess, he started looking for but couldn't find much practical information about what makes projects work. He found instead endless recipes that seemed certain to cause messes like the one he was cleaning up. Between the fantasy that people should be able to accurately estimate novel efforts, the notion of "planning the work and working the plan," and the vacuous idea that on-time, on-budget, on-spec could meaningfully measure success, he concluded that project management theory offered a nearly total lack of real-world utility. "The most popular placebo in business today," he calls it. Nearly a quarter-century of experience hasn't changed David's opinion.

Visit with the smokers outside the building or linger by the water cooler for an extra few minutes and you'll hear no end of rude jokes targeted at the absurd theories, promoted by the Masters, subscribing to the popular but largely disappointing-in-practice cookbook techniques offered by the Project Management Institute, the Software Engineering Institute, and the many consultancies trading on their theories. You'll also hear endless stories of well-intentioned individuals "standing on their own hose complaining about the municipal water pressure." Both the cookbook theorist Masters and their disaffected Slaves combine the wisdom of their experience with the folly of their perspective to create unnecessarily disappointing projects for themselves and for each other.

David remains astounded by how few theorists ever descend to ground level to see what the humans on their projects know will work. He's equally astounded at how few general uprisings muster when an unworkable master plan comes down from above. Every project catastrophe he's seen started when one person decided to exclude the irrelevant-seeming perspective of another person poorly connected to his or her own society. He hopes this book will reassure and instruct those who, like himself, have a job that requires them to make their so-called Masters' projects work anyway, as well as those, also like himself, who are invisibly disaffected Masters overconfidently directing their project communities toward uncertain futures.

In 1993, after fifteen years of dedicated service in the theologic wars, David left Standard Insurance Company's Information Technology Division to join the Ontara Corporation, a pioneer in helping people discover and deploy practical project management techniques. Commuting between his home in Portland, Oregon, and Ontara's Silicon Valley offices, during the next three years David helped design and deliver curious workshops for many of the world's most innovative companies where people fiddled with toys and left more capable of creating high-quality project experiences. In 1996, having fired his boss (it's a long story and he doesn't want to get into it right now), David purchased the sole rights to Ontara's considerable intellectual property and started True North project guidance strategies, Inc. Since then, David has worked to broaden and extend the human productive capability of practicing "project workers," still offering them toys to fiddle with and leaving them capable of productively subverting their Master-Slave relationships. His Mastering Projects Workshop, Mastering Project Work workshop, and BeyondLeadership residential experience introduce unique means for approaching the universal difficulties he first encountered years ago cleaning up that bungled conversion. The hundreds who have graduated from his workshops are the most innovative and adaptive people working on projects today.

David writes, gardens, and occasionally still composes songs in a large Victorian house he shares with his wife and business partner, Amy Schwab, nearly one hundred rose bushes, and two contentious house cats. The house overlooks a tree-lined street in Walla Walla, Washington. David consults and teaches all over the place.

INFORMATION ABOUT THE AUTHOR'S WORKSHOPS AND CONSULTING BUSINESS

True North project guidance strategies, Inc., is a strategic consultancy trading in a human, adaptive approach to project work. David A. Schmaltz fills the role of Principled Consultant, sharing organic techniques well suited to innovative and research-based projects. True North focuses on creating coherence in the real project world. It helps participants to

- Diagnose and creatively resolve difficult issues
- Build communities capable of creating coherent futures
- Move organizations into more community-oriented project cultures

True North offers Brief Consulting™; coaching; mentoring; and client-focused, customized training experiences. True North's workshops include

- Mastering Projects Workshop, designed for project managers and project community members
- Mastering Project Work, designed to help individuals contribute fully in project environments
- BeyondLeadership residential experience, helping leaders teach themselves about creating more effective work lives

True North also operates two Web sites: the Heretics' Forum, a real-time–updatable Web space designed to capture dangerously sane ideas (http://pc.wiki.net); and True North pgs, Inc., Project Community (http://www.projectcommunity.com). True North publishes David's periodic newsletter, *Compass*, and his book *This Isn't a Cookbook*.

You are the most powerful project management tool you will ever use.

Berrett-Koehler Publishers

Berrett-Koehler is an independent publisher of books and other publications at the leading edge of new thinking and innovative practice on work, business, management, leadership, stewardship, career development, human resources, entrepreneurship, and global sustainability.

Since the company's founding in 1992, we have been committed to creating a world that works for all by publishing books that help us to integrate our values with our work and work lives, and to create more humane and effective organizations.

We have chosen to focus on the areas of work, business, and organizations, because these are central elements in many people's lives today. Furthermore, the work world is going through tumultuous changes, from the decline of job security to the rise of new structures for organizing people and work. We believe that change is needed at all levels—individual, organizational, community, and global—and our publications address each of these levels.

To find out about our new books,
special offers,
free excerpts,
and much more,
subscribe to our free monthly eNewsletter at

www.bkconnection.com

Please see next pages for other books
from Berrett-Koehler Publishers

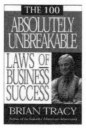
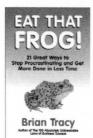

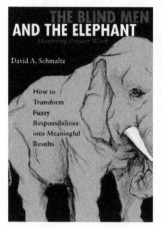